"*Salvation* is a favorite term of Luke's. Nancy Guthrie faithfully and skillfully walks through Acts, showing that God's heart is for all people to be rescued from their greatest enemies: sin and death. Even though Jesus has ascended to the heavens, the life-giving presence of Jesus continues to spread. This is a must-have book as you work through the narrative."

> **Patrick Schreiner**, Associate Professor of New Testament and Biblical Theology, Midwestern Baptist Theological Seminary

"The introduction alone is worth the price of this book, and the book doesn't disappoint. In it you'll find deep nourishment for your soul and experience an increased desire to apply yourself to the study of God's word. With careful exposition and passion, Nancy Guthrie leads us to see our Savior's work in the book of Acts and (to paraphrase her) 'makes us long to live in God's kingdom and experience his power more than ever before.' This book is an invaluable resource for individual or group study."

> **Donna Dobbs**, Women and Children's Ministry Director, First Presbyterian Church, Jackson, Mississippi

"Nancy Guthrie's *Saved* gets at the heart of Acts. Her volume reminds the church of the resurrected Lord sitting on the Father's throne. Christ pours out the Spirit upon believers, and the Spirit ensures the arrival of God's glory to the ends of the earth. What began in the first century continues today, and we must reconsider our calling as it relates to our community and the world around us."

> **Benjamin J. Gladd**, Executive Director, Carson Center for Theological Renewal; series editor, Essential Studies in Biblical Theology

"Nancy Guthrie walks us through the book of Acts, helping us marvel at the big themes and enjoy the unexpected details, all of which come together to give us confidence that as the news of the risen Jesus is proclaimed, God is saving people. Getting to know Acts can be a daunting prospect, especially if you want to teach through it. I'm thrilled to have a resource like this, which I will be turning to on a regular basis."

> **Amy Wicks**, Associate for Women's Discipleship and Pastoral Care, St. Silas Church, Glasgow, United Kingdom

Saved

Saved

Experiencing the Promise of the Book of Acts

Nancy Guthrie

WHEATON, ILLINOIS

Saved: Experiencing the Promise of the Book of Acts

© 2024 by Nancy Guthrie

Published by Crossway
　　　　1300 Crescent Street
　　　　Wheaton, Illinois 60187

Cover design: Crystal Courtney

First printing 2024

Printed in the United States of America

All emphases in Scripture quotations have been added by the author.

Trade paperback ISBN: 978-1-4335-9286-7
ePub ISBN: 978-1-4335-9288-1
PDF ISBN: 978-1-4335-9287-4

Library of Congress Cataloging-in-Publication Data

Names: Guthrie, Nancy, author.
Title: Saved leader's guide : experiencing the promise of the Book of Acts / Nancy Guthrie.
Description: Wheaton, Illinois : Crossway, 2024. | Includes bibliographical references.
Identifiers: LCCN 2023053504 (print) | LCCN 2023053505 (ebook) | ISBN 9781433594915 (trade paperback) | ISBN 9781433594922 (pdf) | ISBN 9781433594939 (epub)
Subjects: LCSH: Bible. Acts—Commentaries. | Christian leadership. | Bible study.
Classification: LCC BS2625.53 .G89 2024 (print) | LCC BS2625.53 (ebook) | DDC 226.607—dc23/eng/20240301
LC record available at https://lccn.loc.gov/2023053504
LC ebook record available at https://lccn.loc.gov/2023053505

Crossway is a publishing ministry of Good News Publishers.

LSC			33	32	31	30	29	28	27	26	25	24
15	14	13	12	11	10	9	8	7	6	5	4	3	2	1

With respect and gratitude, I dedicate this book to some of my female friends who are boldly moving out of their comfort zones to cross significant boundaries with the good news that Jesus saves.

Emanuela Artioli, Coram Deo, Italy
Shamsia Borhani, Afghan refugees around the world
Carol deRossi, Coalición por el Evangelio
Robin Dillard, Servant Group International
Keri Folmar, United Christian Church of Dubai
Jenny Manley, RAK Evangelical Church, United Arab Emirates
Mary Trapnell, Nashville Anti-Human Trafficking Coalition

Contents

Introduction

Acts of the Apostles?

IF YOU THINK ABOUT IT, Acts is kind of a funny name for a book, isn't it? It immediately raises the question, "Whose acts? What acts?"

Of course, the fuller name we find in our English Bibles for this book is Acts of the Apostles. Luke, the author of this book, didn't actually give it that title. It wasn't until the third century that the early church gave it this designation. Why might they have given it that title?

This book certainly tells the story of what happened to and through the twelve apostles and the apostle Paul in the thirty or so years following the death and resurrection of Jesus. It particularly focuses on the ministry of Peter in the first part of the book and then on the ministry of Paul in the second part.

But if this is a book about what the apostles did, it is interesting that after the twelve are listed in the first chapter, we don't hear anything else about most of them, while we have several chapters about the ministries of Stephen and Philip, who were not among the twelve apostles, and Paul, who was added as an apostle. So perhaps providing an account of the actions taken by the apostles was not the primary focus or purpose of Luke's writing.

Acts of the Holy Spirit?

Some have suggested that this book is really about the acts of the Holy Spirit. Certainly the descent of the Holy Spirit is central to this book. It begins with the dramatic descent of the Holy Spirit on the 120 believers gathered in the upper room and Peter's Spirit-empowered sermon in Jerusalem during the feast of Pentecost. From there, the narrative is driven by the expanding circle of those on whom the Spirit descends—on Samaritans (8:17), on Saul (9:17), and on God-fearing Gentiles gathered at the house of Cornelius (10:44; 11:15).

We see the Spirit at work to make the disciples bold in speaking the word of God (4:31), to enable Agabus to foresee a coming famine (11:28), to provide divine instruction and direction (8:29; 11:12; 13:2; 16:6; 19:21; 20:22; 21:4), to provide divine transport (8:39), to comfort God's people (9:31), to provide clarity on the requirements of God (15:28), and to reveal coming persecution (20:23; 21:11). Significantly we see the same Spirit who enabled Jesus to do signs and wonders (2:22) enable his disciples to do signs and wonders again and again throughout the book to authenticate their ministry as being connected to his (2:43; 4:30; 5:12; 6:8; 8:6; 14:3; 15:12; 28:8–9).

We could rightly say that the pouring out of the Holy Spirit on those who put their faith in Christ was a watershed event in human history. Indeed, it marked the dawn of a new age in redemptive history, the dawning of "the last days," the age that stretches from Pentecost until the return of Christ.

Certainly the descent, filling, and work of the Holy Spirit in the book of Acts is important and unique to this book. Yet if we're trying to get at the purpose or aim of the book, we recognize that the descent and indwelling of the Holy Spirit was not an end in itself, but rather served a greater end. What is that end?

Acts of the Preached Word?

When we examine how the Spirit works throughout the book of Acts, we see again and again that the Spirit works through the preached word. Yes, the Spirit speaks and acts directly at numerous points, but most significantly, we see the Spirit working through the means of the preached word of Christ. On the day of Pentecost, the Spirit gave his people the supernatural ability to announce the good news of the gospel of Jesus Christ in languages they didn't know before. Peter preached and the Spirit worked through it, and those who heard were cut to the heart.

So perhaps another possible title for this book could be Acts of the Word. The word almost seems to take on an identity of its own in this book, as it is spreading. The Spirit works through the word to accomplish a work of new creation. Indeed, we could organize the book around the statements of what the word is doing and how it is spreading:

- Immediately following Pentecost we read that three thousand people heard the word preached by Peter and received it (2:41). And from there the word continues to spread.

- The apostles are arrested and beaten and told not to teach. But they do it anyway. And in Acts 6:7 we read, "The word of God continued to increase, and the number of the disciples multiplied greatly in Jerusalem, and a great many of the priests became obedient to the faith."

- Stephen is stoned to death and James is killed by the sword, but we read in Acts 12:24, "The word of God increased and multiplied."

- Saul and Barnabas make Antioch their headquarters, and we read, "The word of the Lord was spreading throughout the whole region" (13:49).

- In his second missionary journey, Paul and Silas go to farther-out places, "so the word of the Lord continued to increase and prevail mightily" (19:20).

- When we come to the end of the book, Paul has faced storm and shipwreck, and he is imprisoned in Rome, facing execution. And what does he do? "From morning till evening he expounded to them, testifying to the kingdom of God and trying to convince them about Jesus both from the Law of Moses and from the Prophets" (28:23).

So the book of Acts is about the acts of the apostles, the acts of the Spirit, and very much about the acts of the preached word. But there is yet another option to consider as a possible title.

Acts of the Enthroned Lord Jesus?

In the first verse of Acts, Luke writes, "In the first book, O Theophilus, I have dealt with all that Jesus *began* to do and teach" (1:1). In his Gospel, Luke wrote about the incarnation, death, and resurrection of Jesus. Implied in his statement is that in this second part of his two-part work, the book of Acts, he is going to present what Jesus *continued* to do and teach.

This means that the transition from Luke to Acts is not from what Jesus did to what the apostles did. Rather, the transition is from what Jesus did while on earth to what Jesus continued to do from heaven. So perhaps another alternative title for this book could be, Acts of the Enthroned Lord Jesus.[1] As we read through the book of Acts, the Lord

---

1 One of the books I found most helpful in writing this book is *The Acts of the Risen Lord Jesus* by Alan J. Thompson (Grand Rapids, MI: InterVarsity Press, 2013). Another is *In the Fullness of Time* by Richard B. Gaffin Jr. (Wheaton, IL: Crossway, 2022), who, in discussing the title of the book of Acts, suggests, "'Acts of the Exalted Christ through the Apostles,' or, going all out (in quasi seventeenth-century Puritan style), 'Acts of the Exalted Christ by the Holy Spirit in the Church as Founded by Him through the Apostles,'" 59.

Jesus is at the center of the action. We hear him calling to himself those who are far off (2:39); adding new believers to his church (2:47; 11:21); sending his angel to open prison doors (5:19; 12:11); providing direction to his disciples (8:26; 9:11); appearing to Stephen and Saul (7:59–60; 9:17); speaking to Saul (9:5, 18:9; 23:11), to Cornelius (10:4), and to Peter (10:14); striking down those who persecute his people (12:23); opening the hearts of hearers of God's word (16:14); and appointing ministers of his word (20:24).

We can never think that Jesus is unconcerned or uninvolved in the affairs of his people and the spread of his gospel. The heart of Jesus is still with his people. The hand of Jesus is still at work among his people.

But, we might ask, at work to accomplish what? The risen and enthroned Lord Jesus is at work by his Spirit giving his apostles boldness to preach, adding to their number, equipping them to establish churches. But to what end? We're left, once again, searching for the deeper purpose toward which the apostles, the Spirit, the word, and the enthroned Lord Jesus are acting.

God's Plan of Salvation Being Carried Out

Perhaps we find help with this by looking at the bookends to Luke's two-volume work. One bookend is Luke's birth narrative of Jesus, where we are told numerous times that the child Mary is carrying is the one who will "give knowledge of salvation to his people" (Luke 1:77). When Simeon takes the baby Jesus into his arms, he praises God saying, "My eyes have seen your salvation" (2:30). In Luke 3, Luke quotes Isaiah 40:3–5 and says that "all flesh shall see the salvation of God" (3:6). The other bookend is Acts 28:28. After quoting Isaiah 6:9–10, Paul proclaims, "Therefore let it be known to you that this salvation of God has been sent to the Gentiles; they will listen." In between these two bookends, we're told that the content of the message that the apostles have been empowered by the Spirit to declare is "the message of salvation" (Acts 13:26), or "the way of salvation" (16:17). Peter declares,

"There is salvation in no one else, for there is no other name under heaven given among men by which we must be saved" (4:12). So, if we wanted to capture what the whole of the book of Acts is about in a sentence, perhaps one way to say it would be this: *The enthroned Lord Jesus is at work by his Spirit through his apostles who are preaching the word, taking the gospel to every nation, and it is accomplishing its intended purpose: people are being saved.*

No other Gospel writer uses the word *saved* and its various forms as much as Luke. In the book of Acts, he uses *saved,* or some form of it, twenty-one times.[2] Indeed, salvation is at the heart of the promise of the book of Acts, the promise that we want to experience for ourselves and for everyone we love. And that is: "Everyone who calls upon the name of the Lord will be saved" (2:21). What generosity of grace!

But what does it really mean to be saved or to experience salvation? In the Old Testament, salvation was about deliverance, preservation, and rescue from enemies. Moses told the people cornered and scared on the shores of the Red Sea that they should "fear not, stand firm, and see the salvation of the LORD, which he will work for you today" (Ex. 14:13). They were saved from the Egyptian army when the Lord rolled back the waters of the Red Sea. But as the Bible's story progresses, we begin to see that the salvation he worked for this one nation throughout the Old Testament was really a shadow of a far greater and more pervasive salvation he intends to work for people from every nation.

The Bible is a book that recounts the work of God accomplishing his great purpose for history: to save his people from their greatest enemies, sin and death, and deliver them into the safety and rest of his presence. In the Gospels we see how God is working for the salvation of his people through the incarnation, Jesus's sinless life, his death, and his resurrection. And in the book of Acts we see how the Lord Jesus is continuing to work out God's eternal plan of salvation for his people

---

2   Patrick Schreiner, *Acts,* Christian Standard Commentary (Nashville, TN: B&H, 2022), 21.

through his ascension, his session as he sits at God's right hand ruling over and interceding for us, and in pouring out his Spirit at Pentecost. We also discover that "his people" includes people from every nation, of every culture and race. God intends to save a people for himself made up of people "from every tribe and language and people and nation" (Rev. 5:9). We await the final great work of salvation to come, when the Lord Jesus will return to destroy his enemies and usher in the new creation. On that day we will experience salvation in all of its glorious fullness.

I wonder how the realization that salvation is at the heart of the story Luke is going to tell us in the book of Acts hits you. Oh, I hope it doesn't make you yawn and think, "Yeah, salvation, I've taken care of that. Let's move on." Instead, I hope the recognition that Acts is most profoundly about the salvation of God will generate in you at least three responses.

First, I hope you'll say, "I have a vested interest in this 'salvation of God.' In fact it's my only hope. I am in need of salvation." For some, this may mean that for the first time you will recognize that you are an outsider to this salvation. Perhaps you will realize that you need to be rescued from sin, forgiven, restored, reconciled. What Acts clearly shows us is that God is not sitting back waiting for you to find him or figure things out. He is at work in his world by his Spirit through his people to make known that salvation is available to you, no matter who you are or what you've done. God is a God who loves to save! He is actively in pursuit of people in need of his salvation.

Others of you may find that you need to adjust your understanding of salvation. Rather than solely pointing back to a day in your past that you "got saved," perhaps Acts will help you to adjust your understanding of this salvation of God to see its past, present, and future manifestations so that you can say, "I have been saved; I am being saved; and I will be saved." I pray this study of Acts will restore to you the joy of your salvation (Ps. 51:12).

Perhaps this study will also cause you to say, "I don't want to settle for being saved myself. I need to have my heart expanded, my vision enlarged, maybe even the purpose toward which I'm investing the ordinary days of my life redirected, as I gain a more thorough understanding of how God is working out his salvation purposes in the era in which I am living."

Second, I hope you'll say, "I want to experience the power of the Holy Spirit as presented in Acts." I pray, as we work our way through Acts, that you will long for the Holy Spirit to work in you and through you as you see the vibrancy of his work among the first believers in Christ. The Spirit's work in and through us likely won't look exactly like what we see in Acts. What is recorded for us in the book of Acts concerns a unique period of redemptive history. Just as we do not anticipate that the crucifixion or resurrection will be repeated, we do not anticipate the events of Pentecost will be repeated. In Acts, we're given a record of a unique time in redemptive history when the Spirit was at work to establish Christ's church throughout the world through the witness of the apostles. But the same Spirit that worked in and through them is still at work in us. The Spirit can empower us to change, empower us to pray, empower us to obey, empower us to proclaim to all who will listen, "Believe in the Lord Jesus, and you will be saved" (16:31).

Third, I hope you'll say, "I believe the tool that the Spirit used in the book of Acts is the same tool he uses today—the word of God. And because of that, I want to hear the word, receive it, submit to it, share it. I want it to increase in my own heart, and I want to have a part in the word of God increasing and multiplying in my home, in my city, in my generation, in the world."

Many of us long to have a sense that God is really at work in our lives. We want more than to merely go through the motions of church attendance. We want a fresh vibrancy to our walk with Christ, fresh insights into who he is and what he is doing in the world. What we need to know is that God has a particular means through which he accomplishes his work of creating newness in the world and in our lives. He works through his word. It is usually slow rather than instant. It is more often ordinary rather than dramatic. But it is certain. I can promise you that as you lean in to listen to what he has to say, as you chew on it, tease out its implications, as you ask it questions and find answers to your questions, God will be at work in your life, remaking you from the inside.

To help you to really work this word into your life over the course of this study, I've prepared a series of personal Bible study questions that I hope you'll complete before you read each chapter in this book. The companion *Saved Personal Bible Study* on the complete text of Acts is available as a download and in a printed version.[1] Do you find it hard to find the time to invest in doing something like that? Can I suggest that you carve out time on Sunday, the Lord's Day, to spend in his word? Maybe you don't typically work through questions on the text of the Bible because you find it difficult. Two heads are better than one. Is there someone you could get together with to work through the questions? Here's the purpose of the questions: to get you into the text before you take in what I have to say about it, to get you thinking and asking questions that hopefully I will answer in what I've written. I want you to be familiar with the facts of the text, but more than that, I want you to invest some thought in seeking to grasp the bigger picture and the *why* behind what we are reading.

Why do we want to invest ourselves in studying Acts? Aren't the stories from this book that some of us learned in Sunday school good enough? (I do wish I still had that salt map of Paul's missionary journeys that I made in vacation Bible school.) We want to see how those stories fit into the larger story of the way God is working out his salvation purposes in the world. We want the power that only comes as the

---

1   The *Saved Personal Bible Study* is available to download or to purchase at Crossway.org.

Spirit works through his word in the interior of our lives. We want the salvation at the center of this book to become the joy and longing of our hearts. We want to revel in the reality that we have been saved; we are being saved; and we will, one day, be fully and finally saved. So, let's study Acts.[2]

---

2 You will find that in a few of these chapters, out of a desire to keep this book to a manageable length, I don't have space to cover every part of the biblical text. I didn't want to make this book about the longest book in the New Testament too long. But I do hope you'll at least read through all of the text yourself. If you work your way through the companion personal Bible study, you will find that it covers all of the text of the book of Acts.

PART 1

SALVATION IN JERUSALEM

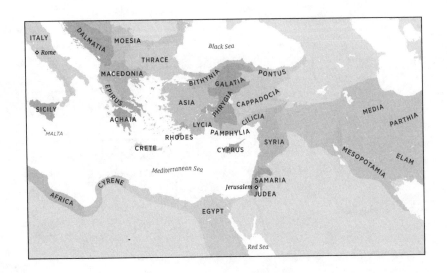

1

You Will Be My Witnesses

Acts 1:1–26

IS THERE AN EVENT OR A SEASON in your life that you can look back on and say, "That changed the course of my life"? I can think of a number of those events or seasons in my own life.

The first chapter of Acts covers a period of fifty days—fifty days that changed the course of the lives of the 120 followers of Jesus who spent these days together. Most significantly, it changed the course of the lives of the twelve apostles of Jesus, who were among those 120 people. And I don't think it's an exaggeration to suggest that what took place in those fifty days also had a significant impact on the course of your life if you are a follower of Christ.

- The resurrection of Jesus, which happened on the first of those fifty days, is what gives you hope that this life is not all there is, and that you follow a living Savior.

- The forty days Jesus spent with the apostles, opening their minds to understand how to rightly read the Old Testament and preparing them to explain it in the pages of the New

Testament, is what provided the gospel witness that the Spirit used to draw you to Christ.

- The fortieth day, when Jesus ascended to the right hand of God the Father in heaven, where he rules over all things, is what gives you confidence that everything that happens in your life is purposeful and working together for your good and for his glory. His promise as he ascended that he will return the same way situates your life in a grand story of future glory.

- The selection of a replacement for Judas so that there were twelve apostles provided the foundation for the new community in which you find your home and identity as a partaker of the new covenant.

What took place during those fifty days is significant, not just for those we read about in the pages of Acts, but also for us. So let's work our way through Acts 1 to get a better sense of it.

Jesus Continued to Do and Teach

In Luke 1, Luke said that he was writing "an orderly account" of the life, death, and resurrection of Jesus based on eyewitness testimony so that his audience, Theophilus, could have certainty about the things he had been taught. He summarizes the content of the Gospel of Luke in the first verse of Acts:

In the first book, O Theophilus, I have dealt with all that Jesus began to do and teach until the day when he was taken up, after he had given commands through the Holy Spirit to the apostles whom he had chosen. (1:1–2)

This implies that what he intends to present in the book of Acts is a fully reliable account of all that Jesus *continued* to do and teach. Though Jesus has ascended to heaven, Luke wants Theophilus and the rest of his readers, including you and me, to know that Jesus has not stopped working and teaching his people. In this book Luke is going to tell us what Jesus continued to do and teach from his throne in heaven.

Jesus Appeared to Them Alive

Luke writes that Jesus "presented himself alive to them after his suffering by many proofs, appearing to them during forty days, and speaking about the kingdom of God" (1:3). That word *alive* is significant. The apostles are not merely to be witnesses to his ministry, his teaching, and his death. He wants us to know that they saw him alive after his death. He did not simply appear to them as a ghostly figure or spirit. He's human. And he's alive. Over forty days Jesus presented "many proofs" of the genuineness of his resurrection that filled them with confidence. These followers were privileged to see and hear and touch the physical body of the resurrected Lord Jesus.

Jesus Taught Them about the Kingdom

Luke writes that during the forty days he appeared to them, he was "speaking about the kingdom of God." They were enrolled in a course of study, The Kingdom of God 101, taught by the King himself. In some ways these early verses of Acts overlap with the final verses of Luke's Gospel, where he gives us a bit more detail about the syllabus for this Kingdom of God 101 class.

The text for the class was the Old Testament. How do we know that? From what we read about these forty days at the end of Luke's Gospel:

Then he said to them, "These are my words that I spoke to you while I was still with you, that everything written about me in the Law of

Moses and the Prophets and the Psalms must be fulfilled." Then he opened their minds to understand the Scriptures, and said to them, "Thus it is written, that the Christ should suffer and on the third day rise from the dead, and that repentance for the forgiveness of sins should be proclaimed in his name to all nations, beginning from Jerusalem." (Luke 24:44–47)

And they couldn't help but understand it like never before because their teacher "opened their minds to understand" the ways in which what they read in the Old Testament was about Christ, specifically about his death and resurrection. He even opened their minds to see how the task he was about to set before them—proclaiming this good news to all nations—had always been a part of God's plan according to the Old Testament.

In "speaking about the kingdom," perhaps Jesus pointed to the kingdom of Israel that took shape in the writings of Moses and throughout the History Books of the Old Testament, and explained the ways in which the nation of Israel was a preview or precursor to a far greater kingdom that will be made up of people from every nation. Surely Jesus must have talked about the fact that he was the promised Son of David, and how many things David wrote about in the psalms were most profoundly about him, because we're going to hear Peter interpret two psalms that way later in Acts. As Jesus worked his way through the prophets who wrote about what the kingdom would be like when God's king would come and establish his rule on the earth, surely Jesus connected those kingdom realities of peace and provision, security and authority, to the previews he had given to them in the miracles he had performed during his three years of earthly ministry. And surely he talked to them about the future of his kingdom, when what he taught them to pray for—"Your kingdom come, your will be done, on earth as it is in heaven" (Matt. 6:10)—will become the reality we will live in for all eternity.

Jesus Told Them to Wait for the Promise of the Father

Over those forty days, as they grew in their understanding of the kingdom of God, I imagine that there must have been a sense of "What do we do now? How do we get started?" And, fortunately, Jesus told them exactly what they needed to do. They needed to wait. Luke records:

> And while staying with them he ordered them not to depart from Jerusalem, but to wait for the promise of the Father, which, he said, "you heard from me; for John baptized with water, but you will be baptized with the Holy Spirit not many days from now." (1:4–5)

What are they waiting for? They're waiting for "the promise of the Father." What had the Father promised? The prophet Joel described a day when God would pour out his Spirit on all flesh (Joel 2:28). God's people had longed for that day. Indeed numerous Old Testament passages indicated that the Father's gift of the Spirit would be an indication of the arrival of a new era when God would establish his king and kingdom (Isa. 32:1; Ezek. 39:29; Joel 2:28–29).[1] The night before he was crucified, Jesus had said to this same group, "But the Helper, the Holy Spirit, whom the Father will send in my name, he will teach you all things and bring to your remembrance all that I have said to you" (John 14:26).

This is what the Father has promised: the pouring out, or the baptism, of the Holy Spirit. Up to this point in redemptive history, the Spirit had been among his people and had occasionally filled a particular individual for a particular task. But God was promising something different. The Spirit's work and power in and among his people, which had been like the trickle of a stream throughout the Old Testament era, would become like Niagara Falls.

---

1   G. K. Beale and D. A. Carson, *Commentary on the New Testament Use of The Old Testament* (Grand Rapids, MI: Baker Academic, 2009), 528.

The forty days of listening to Jesus speak about the kingdom of God must have made all who were enrolled in the class long to live in that kingdom and experience this power more than ever before, which led them to ask Jesus a question:

> So when they had come together, they asked him, "Lord, will you at this time restore the kingdom to Israel?" (1:6)

What did they mean by "restore the kingdom to Israel"? It could be that they were simply longing for Jewish autonomy from the Romans. Certainly that was the expectation of the Messiah that a majority of the Jews shared. But these disciples have just spent forty days immersed in the writing of Moses and the prophets, so it seems more likely that they were longing for the kind of kingdom restoration that the prophets wrote about. The prophets repeatedly spoke of a day when the twelve tribes of Israel, who had been separated when the northern kingdom split from the southern kingdom, would be regathered and restored to God and each other. A regathered and restored Israel would be a beacon of light beckoning the nations to stream to Mount Zion to worship the one true God (Isa. 11; 60; Ezek. 37:16–19). The prophets wrote of a future kingdom that would be garden-like in its atmosphere and abundance. It would be perfectly peaceful, completely secure, and pervasively righteous. Surely their understanding of what this would be like developed over forty days with the risen Jesus and caused them to long for what God promised in a greater way. Who wouldn't want that kind of kingdom to come right now? I do!

Or perhaps it was Jesus's telling them that the Holy Spirit would come "not many days from now" that prompted the question. Throughout the Old Testament, the coming of the Spirit was always a part of "the last days" (Isa. 44:3, 5; Ezek. 36:27). And Jesus had confirmed to them that the last days were upon them.

So how did Jesus answer their question? Or maybe we should ask, Did Jesus answer their question?

> He said to them, "It is not for you to know times or seasons that the Father has fixed by his own authority. But you will receive power when the Holy Spirit has come upon you, and you will be my witnesses in Jerusalem and in all Judea and Samaria, and to the end of the earth." (1:7–8)

In his answer, Jesus seems to shift their orientation away from *when* the kingdom will come toward *how* and *where* and *to whom* it is going to come. Rather than coming in an instant, it's going to come over a period of time that only the Father knows. It is going to come as the testimony of these apostles is used throughout the world to call people of every nation to bow to Jesus as King and thereby enter into his kingdom.

Yes, it is going to be for Israel, but not Israel alone. It is going to be for people from all nations. Jesus wants to expand their grasp of and expectations for what his kingdom is going to be like and who will be included in it. Dennis Johnson explains it this way: "Their concept of restoration needed to be expanded to worldwide, even cosmic, dimensions. . . . They needed to see the expanding horizons of the Lord's work of rescue, repair, and restoration, embracing not only Israelites, but all peoples, in a triumphant conquest of grace."[2]

Jesus Said They Would Be His Witnesses

Central in this passage, in the second part of his answer to their question, is Jesus's statement: "But you will receive power when the Holy Spirit has come upon you, and you will be my witnesses in Jerusalem and in all Judea and Samaria, and to the end of the earth" (1:8). This statement, in fact, provides an outline for the whole book of Acts. In

2 Dennis E. Johnson, *The Message of Acts in the History of Redemption* (Phillipsburg, NJ: P&R, 1997), 35.

chapter 2, these first followers receive power when the Holy Spirit comes upon them, and they begin to preach in Jerusalem (chapters 2–7). From there they will witness to Christ outside of Jerusalem in Judea and in Samaria (chapters 8–11). Then, from chapter 12 on, Paul and others will take the gospel throughout Asia Minor, Asia, and all the way to Rome, the ends of the earth in his day.

But for now, let's focus in on the part of this statement in which Jesus says to them, "You will be my witnesses." I grew up in a tradition in which "witnessing" was something that every Christian was expected to do. It was a general term for telling someone about Jesus or perhaps sharing my "personal testimony" about becoming a Christian. But when Jesus says to this group that they will be his witnesses, he actually means something different. To get the sense of what Jesus means, we need to think about how this term is used in context of a courtroom. A witness in a courtroom is someone who testifies to what he saw and heard firsthand. Since you and I didn't live in the first century and didn't see Jesus after he was raised from the dead with our human eyes, we can never be witnesses to his resurrection in the way Jesus meant when he told these first followers that they would be his witnesses.

That means that we can't apply this statement directly to ourselves. Jesus is not pleading with you and me here to be his witnesses. Rather, Jesus is announcing that God has appointed the eleven (soon to be twelve) apostles to witness to what they saw and heard. Notice that Jesus doesn't *ask* them to be witnesses or even *command* them to be witnesses. He simply *announces* that they *will be* his witnesses.

Think back to what Jesus said during his earthly ministry: "I will build my church, and the gates of hell shall not prevail against it" (Matt. 16:18). What we see in Acts is how that building of his church is going to come about. It will be built as the Holy Spirit comes upon the twelve apostles, and later upon Paul, enabling and empowering them to witness to what they saw and heard from Jesus himself. The

Daniel

apostles are the divinely commissioned eyewitnesses to the life, death, resurrection, and, as we're about to see, the ascension of Jesus Christ.

But does that mean that there is nothing here for us to do? Absolutely not! In the Gospels and Epistles of the New Testament, we have the record of what these reliable witnesses saw and heard and were taught by Jesus. Our role is to proclaim what these witnesses saw and heard and were taught from the Scriptures. We are to proclaim the gospel according to the apostles as recorded in the New Testament. We are to hold fast to the gospel they proclaimed rather than embellish or alter it. And in the same way that they were dependent on the Holy Spirit to make their witness effective, so we are to be completely dependent on the Holy Spirit to use our proclamation of the gospel to bring those who hear it into the kingdom of King Jesus.

Jesus Ascended to Heavenly Glory

Perhaps the apostles were still processing the implications of Jesus's answer to their question when, "as they were looking on, he was lifted up, and a cloud took him out of their sight" (1:9). Having spent the previous forty days in the Old Testament scriptures, when they saw Jesus lifted up to heaven in a cloud of glory, surely they immediately thought about the vision given to the prophet Daniel, who saw that "with the clouds of heaven there came one like a son of man, and he came to the Ancient of Days and was presented before him. And to him was given dominion and glory and a kingdom, that all peoples, nations, and languages should serve him" (Dan. 7:13–14).

What Daniel foresaw in a vision from heaven's perspective, these disciples now saw in history from the perspective of earth. Jesus, the Son of Man, ascended with the clouds into the heavenly throne room where his Father gave him dominion and glory and an everlasting kingdom. This was his coronation day as King. Indeed, as the apostles considered the instructions they had just been given by Jesus in light of what Daniel wrote about the expansive nature of his kingdom in this Daniel 7 passage, it must have been increasingly clear to them that the kingdom of Jesus was not simply a kingdom for Jewish people. Rather, it was a kingdom for "all people, nations, and languages." This is why Jesus had appeared to and taught them, and why he was going to send his Spirit to them. They were going to be his witnesses so that people from every nation would become a part of his glorious eternal kingdom. The apostle's lives were filled with purpose and significance and confidence that their king had not abandoned them, but would empower them for their mission until the day when he descends in the same glorious way they saw him ascend.

Jesus Chose a Twelfth Apostle

From a magnificent scene of heavenly glory, Luke seems to plunge us as readers into what may seem like a mundane list of names followed by a gruesome account of the death of Judas. Consider that many things must have happened and been discussed during the ten days that followed the ascension of Jesus, and this is the one thing he recorded. If this is the one thing he recorded, then we need to try to grasp its significance.

> Then they returned to Jerusalem from the mount called Olivet, which is near Jerusalem, a Sabbath day's journey away. And when they had entered, they went up to the upper room, where they were staying, Peter and John and James and Andrew, Philip and Thomas, Bartholomew and Matthew, James the son of Alphaeus and Simon the Zealot and Judas the son of James. All these with one accord were devoting themselves to prayer, together with the women and Mary the mother of Jesus, and his brothers. (1:12–14)

Earlier in his Gospel, Luke recorded that Jesus "called his disciples and chose from them twelve, whom he named apostles" (Luke 6:13). The picture is of a large number of disciples following him, and from that large group of followers, Jesus chose twelve that he named as apostles. Why would Jesus specifically choose twelve to be named as apostles? Israel as a nation had been built on the foundation of the twelve tribes of Israel. To be a part of God's people was to be connected to these twelve tribes. I imagine that as Jesus spent those forty days speaking about the kingdom, he had talked about how God had set his love on those twelve tribes and how those twelve tribes had rejected God's covenant. Jesus had come as the mediator of a better covenant and to establish a new people of God. He had said to his apostles the night before he was crucified, "I assign to you, as my Father assigned to me, a kingdom, that you may eat and drink at my table in my kingdom and sit on thrones judging the twelve tribes of Israel" (Luke 22:29–30). In other words, Jesus's kingdom would not be founded on the bloodline of the twelve sons of Jacob but rather on the gospel witness of the twelve apostles.

Following Jesus's ascension as they waited in the upper room, perhaps still poring over the Old Testament scriptures, Peter realized that there was a problem. Because of the betrayal and death of Judas, there were now only eleven apostles. Evidently the forty days of having their minds opened by Jesus to understand the Scriptures was effective. As Peter read Psalms 69 and 109, he recognized that some things that David wrote about himself and his enemies were more profoundly about Jesus and his enemy, Judas:

In those days Peter stood up among the brothers (the company of persons was in all about 120) and said, "Brothers, the Scripture had to be fulfilled, which the Holy Spirit spoke beforehand by the mouth of David concerning Judas, who became a guide to those who arrested Jesus. For he was numbered among us and was allotted his share in this ministry." (Now this man acquired a field with the reward of his wickedness, and falling headlong he burst open in the middle and all his bowels gushed out. And it became known to all the inhabitants of Jerusalem, so that the field was called in their own language Akeldama, that is, Field of Blood.)

"For it is written in the Book of Psalms,

'May his camp become desolate,
    and let there be no one to dwell in it'" (1:15–20a; cf.
        Ps. 69:25)

Luke includes the gory details about Judas's death because they help connect Judas to the curses mentioned in Psalm 69, an imprecatory psalm that pronounces a curse on the life and the land of the evildoer who opposes God's king. Peter sees in the way and the place where Judas died that he died under God's curse for his treachery against God's King, Jesus.

Peter goes on to apply another curse against an opponent of God's king in Psalm 109 to Judas:

"Let another take his office." (1:20b; cf. Ps. 109:8)

Peter concludes from reading the Psalms, in the way that Jesus spent forty days teaching his disciples to read them, that Judas needed to be replaced. But Peter had no interest in picking the replacement himself. Just as Jesus chose the initial twelve, including, in his sovereignty, one that would betray him, so Jesus had to choose the one who would replace him. They surveyed the 120 people who were gathered in the room to determine who had the proper qualifications. It had to be someone who had been with Jesus from the time John baptized Jesus through the forty days of being enrolled in his kingdom classroom. And there were two among them who fit the requirements—Justus and Matthias. How would they choose? They prayed and asked Jesus to show them whom he had chosen. And when the dice were rolled and landed on Matthias, they recognized him as Jesus's choice. They were again complete as the twelve, ready and waiting for the empowerment of the Holy Spirit to witness to Jesus for the rest of their lives, at the cost of their lives.

These twelve apostles formed the foundation of Jesus's new community. Paul will write to the Gentile believers in Ephesus that they have become "fellow citizens with the saints and members of the household of God . . . , Christ Jesus himself being the cornerstone" (Eph. 2:20). And John will record his vision of the new Jerusalem as a city with twelve foundations and on which are written the twelve names of the twelve apostles of the Lamb (Rev. 21:14).

This is why what happened during these fifty days has an impact on the course your life will take. If you have believed the witness of those twelve apostles and have thereby taken hold of the Christ they testify to by faith, then one day you're going to make your home in the new Jerusalem, the eternal city of God. I imagine the twelve apostles will still be testifying not only to the life, death, resurrection, and ascension of Jesus, but at that point they'll also be able to testify that Jesus really did return in the same way as they saw him go into heaven. Perhaps we'll hear them say, "Finally the time has come. The Lord has, at *this* time, fully restored his kingdom. He's brought all his people in. And he will reign forever and ever."

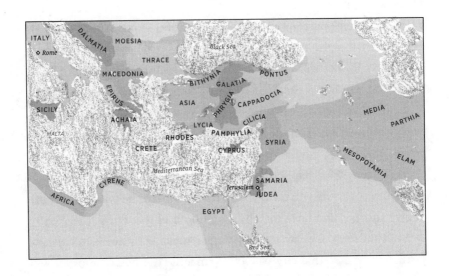

I Will Pour Out My Spirit

Acts 2:1–47

MY MOM GREW UP on a farm in southeast Missouri. Our family made regular trips to the farm while I was growing up. My older sister loved the farm. She wanted to spend as many weeks there in the summer as she possibly could. She loved spending all day riding on the combine, the huge machine that would separate the grain from everything else, and then emptying the harvested grain into a cart or silo. Me, not so much. It was hot, hard work.

Rain was a constant topic of conversation on the farm—how long it has been since it rained, when it might rain, not enough rain, too much rain. If the rain didn't come, there was no growth and therefore no harvest. And when the rain came, there was growth and harvest.

If we look back into the Old Testament, we see that rain is a constant topic in the Bible. God made it clear to his people, as they prepared to enter the land that he was giving them, that he is the source of the rain. They were to celebrate his provision of rain at the very beginning of the harvest by offering him the firstfruits of their harvest. Fifty days after the Feast of Passover, they were to celebrate the Feast of

Pentecost. At this feast they were to wave before the Lord two loaves of bread made from newly harvested choice flour.

Now, we know that Jesus fulfilled the Feast of Passover when he was √offered as a spotless lamb. So did Jesus fulfill the Feast of Pentecost? And if so, how? We'll explore that. But first, let's work our way through Acts 2, seeking to answer three questions it raises (two of which we find in the text itself): (1) What happened? (2) What does this mean? and (3) What do we do? Then we'll come back to see how the events of that particular day of Pentecost fulfilled what the feast God's people celebrated over the centuries had been pointing to all along.

fulfill?,

What Happened?

When we left off at the end of Acts 1, 120 disciples of Jesus, including his family and the twelve apostles, were gathered in the upper room, likely the second floor of a large home in Jerusalem. We're told they were "devoting" themselves to prayer. There was an intensity and desperation to their prayers as they followed Jesus's instructions to "wait for the promise of the Father" (1:4).

> When the day of Pentecost arrived, they were all together in one place. And suddenly there came from heaven a sound like a mighty rushing wind, and it filled the entire house where they were sitting. And divided tongues as of fire appeared to them and rested on each one of them. And they were all filled with the Holy Spirit and began to speak in other tongues as the Spirit gave them utterance. (2:1–4)

We could say that rain came. The Spirit was poured out on God's people like rain. There was the sound of wind, but no actual wind. And there was a sign—tongues "as of fire"—so something that presented like fire. Wind and fire often marked unique times throughout redemptive history when heavenly and earthly realms came together. The Lord spoke from the whirlwind to Job (Job 38:1), fire came down from heaven when the glory of the Lord filled the temple in Jerusalem (2 Chron. 7:1), fire from God fell on Elijah's sacrifices (1 Kings 18:38), and the glory of God appeared to Ezekiel as fire and brightness that arrived on a stormy wind (Ezek. 1:4). John the Baptist had said that while he baptized with water, one who would come would "baptize . . . with the Holy Spirit and fire" (Luke 3:16). Here was that Holy Spirit and fire.

And this wasn't just fire; it was fire in the form of tongues. Why might that be? Because the Spirit was working a miracle of speech among them. The Spirit was empowering them to do something with their own tongues. These tongues as of fire came down to rest on each of the 120 believers in the room, and suddenly these largely uneducated Galileans who spoke Aramaic and Greek were able to articulate the truth of the gospel of Christ in the languages of all the various people groups who had gathered in Jerusalem for the feast.

> Now there were dwelling in Jerusalem Jews, devout men from every nation under heaven. And at this sound the multitude came together, and they were bewildered, because each one was hearing them speak in his own language. (2:5–6)

These were devout Jews, and Gentiles who had become Jewish converts, who lived throughout the known world.

> "Parthians and Medes and Elamites and residents of Mesopotamia, Judea and Cappadocia, Pontus and Asia, Phrygia and Pamphylia, Egypt and the parts of Libya belonging to Cyrene, and visitors from Rome, both Jews and proselytes, Cretans and Arabians—we hear them telling in our own tongues the mighty works of God." (2:9–11)

Many of them had traveled to Jerusalem for the Feast of Pentecost. Because they were "devout," we can assume that they had been praying for God to fulfill all the promises of the Old Testament. And then suddenly one of these 120 believers began to explain to them, in their own language, how God had accomplished his promises in the life, death, resurrection, and ascension of Jesus.

The apostles had been told that they were to be witnesses to Jerusalem and to Judea and Samaria and to the ends of the earth. Certainly they must have been wondering how that was going to happen. It would have been hard for them to imagine the way in which the one who called them to the task would equip them for the task. And while we can't necessarily expect to hear what they heard, see what they saw, and do what they did, we can expect that the same Jesus by his same Spirit is equipping us for the task he has given to us: to proclaim the gospel that has been handed down to us from these apostolic witnesses.

What Does This Mean?

As you can imagine, people suddenly speaking in other languages was startling, confusing:

And all were amazed and perplexed, saying to one another, "What does this mean?" (2:12)

It's a good question. Peter provided the people gathered that day with the answer in three parts, showing that what was happening fulfilled what the prophet Joel wrote about, what God had always planned, and what David wrote about in the Psalms.

So, first, the prophet Joel. But to help us understand the significance of what Joel said, let's consider something that Moses said. Moses, who is considered the greatest of all prophets, said at one point, "Would that all the LORD's people were prophets, that the LORD would put his Spirit on them!" (Num. 11:29). It was about six hundred years later that Joel recorded his prophecy. And in it, Joel wrote that what Moses desired—that the Spirit would be on all of the Lord's people enabling them all to speak God's word with clarity—would, indeed, happen one day in the future. Here's how Peter quotes Joel's prophecy:

"This is what was uttered through the prophet Joel:

> 'And in the last days it shall be, God declares,
> that I will pour out my Spirit on all flesh,
> and your sons and your daughters shall prophesy,
>> and your young men shall see visions,
>> and your old men shall dream dreams;
> even on my male servants and female servants
>> in those days I will pour out my Spirit, and they shall
>> prophesy.
> And I will show wonders in the heavens above
>> and signs on the earth below,
>> blood, and fire, and vapor of smoke;
> the sun shall be turned to darkness
>> and the moon to blood,
>> before the day of the Lord comes, the great and magnificent
>> day.'" (2:16–20)

So how does this answer their question, What does this mean?

First, Peter is saying that what Joel prophesied has begun. The Spirit has been poured out on ordinary believers.

Up to this point in redemptive history, the Spirit was occasionally poured out on a particular person for accomplishing a particular task. But nowhere in the Old Testament do we read about the Spirit coming to dwell permanently in ordinary believers. Joel prophesied that the day would come when God would reveal himself much more fully to all his people. No one would be left out. And Peter says that day has come. What happened on this day—this Pentecost—became a dividing line of history. Ever since that day, whenever people become joined to Christ by faith, the Holy Spirit comes to dwell within them. If you have taken hold of Christ, the Spirit has sealed you to him and has come to dwell in you.

According to Joel, the result of the Spirit being poured out was that all of God's people would prophesy. In other words, the proclamation of the news of God's salvation would not be the task of a select few but of all who would receive the Spirit. Here in Acts, to be a prophet is to speak "the mighty works of God." It is to tell what God is doing in the world through Jesus Christ to accomplish his great salvation. God's Spirit was poured out on these 120 believers so that they were able to articulate the gospel to those gathered in Jerusalem.

So why has the Spirit been poured out on you and me? The Spirit provides us with the power we need to speak—to each other, to our friends and family, to those we don't know—about who Jesus is and what he has done.

Joel also wrote that when the Spirit was poured out, God's people would see visions and dream dreams. Now what do we do with that?

In the Old Testament, the Lord often spoke to his prophets through visions and dreams. But Pentecost was, once again, a dividing line in history. God spoke to those prophets through dreams and visions because they did not have the Spirit dwelling in them. We do! They did not have the full revelation of God in the person and work of Christ. We do! In the Scriptures we have the authoritative revelation of Jesus Christ as recorded by the apostolic witnesses. And by his Spirit we have everything we need to have Spirit-empowered conversations about Jesus with whoever will listen. We have this incredibly open invitation that we simply must share:

> " 'And it shall come to pass that everyone who calls upon the name of the Lord shall be saved.' " (2:21)

Peter connects the outpouring of the Spirit with the offer of salvation to those who call on the name of the Lord. Everyone is invited in. Salvation is for everyone who will call out to Jesus asking for that salvation.

Peter continued answering their question, "What does this mean?" with a second point. The meaning is that the death and resurrection of Jesus was always God's plan.

This was just a matter of weeks after Jesus had been put to death in Jerusalem. Surely many who were gathered there were still trying to make sense of it along with the rumors they were hearing that he had risen from the dead. Peter wants these Jews gathered in Jerusalem to understand that the Spirit being poured out is the outworking of God's sovereign plan, a plan that included the death and resurrection of Jesus.

> "Men of Israel, hear these words: Jesus of Nazareth, a man attested to you by God with mighty works and wonders and signs that God did through him in your midst, as you yourselves know—this Jesus, delivered up according to the definite plan and foreknowledge of God, you crucified and killed by the hands of lawless men. God raised him up, loosing the pangs of death, because it was not possible for him to be held by it." (2:22–24)

according to God's plan

Peter is connecting what was happening on the day of Pentecost with what happened fifty days before. He's saying that none of it has been an accident; it all fits together to accomplish God's plan from before the foundations of the earth to have a people for himself—a people from every nation of the earth. What they were witnessing was actually a "part of a single, unified complex of events. . . . Without [Pentecost], the work that climaxes in Christ's death and resurrection would be unfinished, incomplete."[1]

So Peter has answered their "What does this mean?" question by presenting, first, Joel's prophecy and, second, God's foreknowledge and plan. Next, he moves on to what David wrote in Psalms 16 and 110. His third point is that, according to David, Jesus is the Christ.

1   Richard B. Gaffin Jr., *Perspectives on Pentecost: Studies in New Testament Teaching on the Gifts of the Holy Spirit* (Phillipsburg, NJ: P&R 1979), 17, 20.

First, Peter goes to Psalm 16 and asserts that when David wrote these words, he could not have been writing about his own experience but was actually writing about the experience of Jesus:

"For David says concerning him,

'I saw the Lord always before me,
    for he is at my right hand that I may not be shaken;
therefore my heart was glad, and my tongue rejoiced;
    my flesh also will dwell in hope.
For you will not abandon my soul to Hades,
    or let your Holy One see corruption.
You have made known to me the paths of life;
    you will make me full of gladness with your presence.'"
        (2:25–28)

Here is the psalmist writing a song, saying, "I am not going to rot in the grave." But, of course, David died and was buried and remains in his tomb. Peter makes the point that David couldn't have been writing about himself and that this song was most profoundly about David's greater Son, the Christ. In quoting from this psalm, Peter wants to draw his listeners' attention to a particular sign that should convince them that Jesus is the Christ: the resurrection. Peter says this while surrounded by the apostles, who were all eyewitnesses to his resurrection. So, in a sense, Peter is saying, "David is a reliable prophetic witness from the past, and we, the twelve apostles, are reliable witnesses in the present."

Peter isn't finished appealing to David to convince his listeners that Jesus is the Christ. Next, Peter uses Psalm 110 to show that Jesus ascended into heaven and has been exalted to the right hand of God himself where he reigns until the day he returns to accomplish the final judgment of his enemies and the final salvation of his people.

"For David did not ascend into the heavens, but he himself says,

'The Lord said to my Lord,
"Sit at my right hand,
until I make your enemies your footstool."'" (2:34–35)

Psalm 110 pictured a divine figure ascending to the right hand of God (there's the ascension of Jesus), seated at his right hand (there's the session of Jesus), until his enemies are crushed (there's the return of Jesus).

At this point in his sermon, Peter comes to the climax, the conclusion his listeners simply must come to based on what he has presented. He says that on the basis of the resurrection, ascension, and enthronement of Jesus, there is something that all who have lived in anticipation of the promises of the prophets becoming reality can and should know with complete certainty:

"Let all the house of Israel therefore know for certain that God has made him both Lord and Christ, this Jesus whom you crucified." (2:36)

This certainty Peter is calling his listeners to, and calling us to, is not arrogant certainty. He's calling us to the kind of certainty that leads us to humble trust, the kind of certainty that causes us to reevaluate what we've been putting our confidence in up to this point and to recognize that Jesus is worthy of our trust, worthy of our lives. This conclusion or certainty he's calling his listeners to is, in one sense, a matter of the mind. Peter has made a clear case to be thought through and evaluated, contending that Jesus is the Christ as promised and prophesied in the Old Testament. But Peter is not merely calling for intellectual agreement. He's calling for a personal response to the truth he has presented. Jesus is Lord. And because of that he should not, indeed he cannot, be resisted or ignored. The reality of the person of Jesus demands a response. And the group in the sound of Peter's voice wants to know how to respond.

> Now when they heard this they were cut to the heart, and said to Peter and the rest of the apostles, "Brothers, what shall we do?" (2:37)

What Do We Do?

"Cut to the heart." The reality of the identity and lordship of Jesus pierced into the deepest parts of their minds, wills, and emotions. They were moved by this reality—so much so that they were willing to do whatever it took to respond rightly to this revelation. Peter was ready with an answer. He told them three things that they needed to do in response to their certainty that God has made Jesus both Lord and Christ:

> Peter said to them, "Repent and be baptized every one of you in the name of Jesus Christ for the forgiveness of your sins, and you will receive the gift of the Holy Spirit." (2:38)

1. Repent and Be Baptized

Repentance has always been and will always be the way into restored fellowship with God. Four more times in the book of Acts, the message of the apostles will be a call to repent. Repentance is turning away from self, away from whatever or whomever we've given our allegiance, and toward Christ. So Peter was calling these Jews and proselytes to turn away from righteousness through law-keeping and temple ritual and to turn toward righteousness through faith in Christ, acceptance of his once-for-all sacrifice.

They were to make a public demonstration of their new allegiance to Christ through water baptism. Peter's instruction to be baptized must have been a bit perplexing, and perhaps a hurdle for some of them. It was a humbling thing for a Jew to say, by submitting to baptism, "Being of Jewish descent simply isn't enough. I can't be saved by that. I need Jesus. I want to immerse myself in who he is and what he has done so that I become fully identified with him and with his new people."

2. Receive Forgiveness and the Gift of the Holy Spirit

This is less about what they needed to do than about what they needed to receive. As they went into the waters of baptism, they could be sure that their sins were being washed away. Forgiven. And they could be sure that the same Holy Spirit who had been poured out on those 120 who had been telling them about Christ in their own language would also be poured out on them. Indeed, the Spirit would continue with them, living in them.

3. Believe That This Salvation Is for You and for Your Children

Peter said, "The promise is for you and for your children and for all who are far off, everyone whom the Lord our God calls to himself" (2:39). He was telling them, and he is telling us: Jesus can change the trajectory of your life and the lives of everyone in your family. So as we consider those we love who have so far refused this repentance and this gift of forgiveness and the Holy Spirit, we pray. We petition the Lord our God to call them to himself. Verse 41 says that "those who received his word" were added to these original 120 believers. So we pray and ask God for Spirit-empowered opportunities for gospel conversation, and then we rely on the Spirit for the courage and clarity we need to articulate the gospel that has been handed down to us by the twelve apostles. We pray and ask God, by his Spirit, to make those who are far off receptive to his word.

Luke records,

So those who received his word were baptized, and there were added that day about three thousand souls. (2:41)

Three thousand people could point to that specific day when they repented, were baptized, and received forgiveness and the gift of the Holy Spirit. That first Pentecost was not only the dividing line of history; it was the dividing line in their lives. There was before and there was after. Their lives were transformed because of the Spirit poured out like rain on Pentecost. They were the firstfruits of a far greater harvest to come.

> And they devoted themselves to the apostles' teaching and the fellowship, to the breaking of bread and the prayers. And awe came upon every soul, and many wonders and signs were being done through the apostles. And all who believed were together and had all things in common. And they were selling their possessions and belongings and distributing the proceeds to all, as any had need. And day by day, attending the temple together and breaking bread in their homes, they received their food with glad and generous hearts, praising God and having favor with all the people. And the Lord added to their number day by day those who were being saved. (2:42–47)

Luke tells us that they became devoted to four things. They were devoted to the apostles' teaching, as they applied what they learned in those forty days with Jesus. They were devoted to fellowship with each other, sharing meals together, including the meal Jesus left them to remember him. They were devoted to praying together. I can't imagine it was merely relegated to mealtime. And they were devoted to taking care of those in need among them. The Spirit poured out on them went to work in them, transforming them into a new community.

We began by talking about the Feast of Pentecost, which was also called the Feast of Harvest. As we see three thousand people added to the number of the 120 people who were gathered in the upper room in prayer, we see how this day fulfilled what this feast, prescribed in Moses's day, had always been pointing toward. It had always been God's intention to use his own special people as instruments to bring in a great harvest of humanity, and that is what began in earnest on the day of Pentecost. God chose the time when people from all over the world would be in Jerusalem to reap a spiritual harvest of three thousand souls for his kingdom, the firstfruits of a far greater harvest to come.

The harvest continues today as the Spirit continues to give ordinary people like you and me everything we need to articulate the gospel to others. Right now, the Lord of the harvest is sending out laborers—you and me—into his field (Luke 10:2). So we go, we speak, we pray for the Spirit's power to rain down, and we look forward to the next big day on the timeline of redemptive history, the day when the Lord of the harvest will come to gather his harvest home.

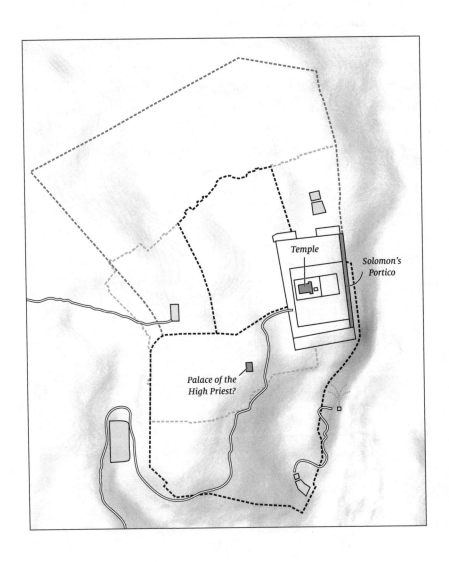

Temple

Solomon's
Portico

Palace of the
High Priest?

3

In Jesus the Resurrection from the Dead

Acts 3:1–4:31

AS I WRITE TODAY, my city, my community, and my friends are reeling from a shooting at one of our Christian schools that took the lives of six people and robbed the school children of innocence. We're weeping over the loss and the trauma. Politicians and pundits are arguing over the root causes and solutions. Ordinary people are trying to make sense of it. This kind of violence and outright evil causes us to ask, "What is this world coming to?" It makes us desperate for a world in which innocence is not robbed and evil does not have the power to destroy and death doesn't have the power to devastate.

When we ask the question, "What is this world coming to?" we might assume that there is no real answer that can be known. But the Bible, including Acts 3–4, offers the most profound answer to the devastating and deadly impact sin has had on the world we live in. We find it in the summary of Peter's sermon, which captures the essence of his message, and it is this: Peter and John were "proclaiming in Jesus the resurrection from the dead" (4:2).

Notice that their message was not simply that Jesus resurrected from the dead. That reality undergirds their message—it was the key piece of evidence they used to develop their argument—but it isn't the point of their message. Nor does it say, "You will rise from the dead." Once again, if you are in Christ, this is true, and it is an aspect of their message, but it isn't the point of their message. Their message is far more all-encompassing.

"The resurrection from the dead" is, in a sense, a technical phrase for the Old Testament anticipation of a day in the future when God's king will reign over his people. All his enemies will be defeated. And all his people will enjoy unending abundance, joy, health, and security. This is the good life lived in the presence of God that Adam failed to lead us into, and the last Adam—Jesus—is going to lead us into.

Most of the Old Testament prophets wrote about the coming reality. The prophet Ezekiel described God's people as being like a valley of dry bones and a day coming when new life will be breathed into those dry bones (Ezek. 37). The prophet Daniel looked ahead to a day when "many of those who sleep in the dust of the earth shall awake, some to everlasting life, and some to shame and everlasting contempt" (Dan. 12:2). Isaiah wrote this about the great day of restoration to come:

Then the eyes of the blind shall be opened,
    and the ears of the deaf unstopped;
then shall the lame man leap like a deer. (Isa. 35:5–6)

All of this means that what Peter and John were essentially saying to those gathered at the temple in Jerusalem on the day we're going to read about in Acts 3 and 4 was: *The resurrection from the dead that the Old Testament scriptures pointed toward, the time of restoration—it has begun. The miracle at the Beautiful Gate demonstrates it.*

The Miracle That Demonstrates It

Let's go back to the beginning of chapter 3, where we read about the miracle at the Beautiful Gate of the temple that, according to Peter and

Miracles   *Beautiful Gate*

John, demonstrates "in Jesus the resurrection from the dead." We just read from Isaiah, who said that when you witness blind people being able to see, deaf people able to hear, and lame people leaping, you'll know that all of God's promises of a future restoration are becoming reality. Over the previous three years, crowds had witnessed these very things taking place in the ministry of Jesus as he healed the blind, the deaf, and the lame. Now the crowds are about to witness the same kinds of miracles in the ministry of Jesus's apostles.

> Now Peter and John were going up to the temple at the hour of prayer, the ninth hour. And a man lame from birth was being carried, whom they laid daily at the gate of the temple that is called the Beautiful Gate to ask alms of those entering the temple. Seeing Peter and John about to go into the temple, he asked to receive alms. And Peter directed his gaze at him, as did John, and said, "Look at us." And he fixed his attention on them, expecting to receive something from them. (3:1–5)

Perhaps this man had stopped looking at those whom he asked for money under a heavy weight of shame. But Peter and John want this man to look at them. He doesn't know it, but his whole life is about to change.

> But Peter said, "I have no silver and gold, but what I do have I give to you. In the name of Jesus Christ of Nazareth, rise up and walk!" (3:6)

They're at the Beautiful Gate, an expansive entrance to the temple complex that is inlaid with silver and gold. And it is as if Peter points at the ornate gate and says to the lame man, "I have something to give you that the temple system will never be able to provide." Peter and John want to give this man something with far more power to change his life than a few coins—the power of the name of Jesus, not as a magical incantation, but as the source of his healing.

And he took him by the right hand and raised him up, and immediately his feet and ankles were made strong. And leaping up, he stood and began to walk, and entered the temple with them, walking and leaping and praising God. And all the people saw him walking and praising God, and recognized him as the one who sat at the Beautiful Gate of the temple, asking for alms. And they were filled with wonder and amazement at what had happened to him. (3:7–10)

Feet and ankles that have never been walked on, that have never borne any weight, are suddenly strong. People have only ever known him as a heap of need, as an object of pity and a recipient of their charity. And he is not just walking. Twice we're told that he's leaping and praising God. This lame man is leaping like a deer! Just like Isaiah said would happen when God would come to save his people.

The Message That Explains It

The commotion is attracting attention. A lot of attention. Evidently thousands of people are gathering around Peter and John and this formerly lame man. Peter uses it as an opportunity to explain what has taken place.

While he clung to Peter and John, all the people, utterly astounded, ran together to them in the portico called Solomon's. And when Peter saw it he addressed the people: "Men of Israel, why do you wonder at this, or why do you stare at us, as though by our own power or piety we have made him walk? The God of Abraham, the God of Isaac, and the God of Jacob, the God of our fathers, glorified his servant Jesus, whom you delivered over and denied in the presence of Pilate, when he had decided to release him. But you denied the Holy and Righteous One, and asked for a murderer to be granted to you, and you killed the Author of life, whom God raised from the dead. To this we are witnesses. And his name—by faith in his name—has made this man strong whom you see and know, and the faith that is through Jesus has given the man this perfect health in the presence of you all." (3:11–16)

Peter wants to be clear that the power to make the lame man walk did not come from them. Where does this power come from? The power is in Jesus. This "perfect health" has been restored in his name, under his authority, by his power. Peter connects the power that raised this lame man to walk to the power that raised Jesus from the dead. It is a power they should be familiar with since they claim to be in relationship with the God of Abraham, Isaac, and Jacob. What they're witnessing is the fulfillment of God's purposes for his people that he had in mind when he called Abraham and the purposes he has been working out through Abraham's descendants ever since.

Did you notice how many times Peter used the word *you* as he spoke to the gathered crowd? It's only been a few weeks since some of these people were in another crowd, demanding that Jesus be crucified. And Peter is not letting them off the hook. We can almost see him pointing the finger: "You delivered him over"; "You denied the Holy and Righteous One"; "You asked for a murderer to be released instead"; "You killed the Author of life."

> "And now, brothers, I know that you acted in ignorance, as did also your rulers. But what God foretold by the mouth of all the prophets, that his Christ would suffer, he thus fulfilled." (3:17–18)

He has been pointing at them, pointing out their culpability for the murder of Jesus. But in reality, what they did was actually a part of God's plan. Indeed, the Old Testament prophets had written that God's King, when he came into the world, would be treated this way. Peter acknowledges that they had not seen that Jesus was God's King. They had not put it together that Jesus fulfilled everything the Old

Testament prophets had written about the coming of the Christ. But they should have known. They should have seen it. Now they have no excuse as he has set it before them plainly. And now that they know, there's something they must do and something they must receive:

> "Repent therefore, and turn back, that your sins may be blotted out, that times of refreshing may come from the presence of the Lord, and that he may send the Christ appointed for you, Jesus, whom heaven must receive until the time for restoring all the things about which God spoke by the mouth of his holy prophets long ago." (3:19–21)

Peter is still saying "you," but he's no longer indicting them; he's speaking grace to them. He's inviting them to get in on everything Jesus came to provide. All *your* sins can be blotted out. *You* can receive the Holy Spirit who will bring wholeness and newness to *your* life.

Peter's explanation for what this miracle of the lame man walking was all about was anchored in a timeline of God's plans for history. This is the time for repentance, he says, as Jesus has ascended into heaven. He's there until the great day of restoration, resurrection, and renewal comes, the day of his return. Peter began with God calling Abraham and worked his way through the earthly and now heavenly ministry of Jesus. And he ends looking forward to the next big event on the timeline of redemptive history, "the time for restoring all . . . things." Now, he says, is the window of opportunity for repentance, forgiveness, and a fresh new experience of communion with God through Christ.

In case they're not yet convinced, Peter begins calling witnesses to the stand to testify to this now-and-not-yet restoration centered *in Jesus*. First, he calls Moses.

> "Moses said, 'The Lord God will raise up for you a prophet like me from your brothers. You shall listen to him in whatever he tells you.

And it shall be that every soul who does not listen to that prophet shall be destroyed from the people.' And all the prophets who have spoken, from Samuel and those who came after him, also proclaimed these days." (3:22–24; cf. Deut. 18:15, 18, 19)

Notice specifically what he says the prophets proclaimed: "these days." What days? The days when the Spirit would be poured out, when the nations would be invited in, when the restoration that God intends to accomplish throughout all of creation would begin in the interior of the lives of all who are in Jesus.

Next Peter calls Abraham to the stand. *Abraham*

"You are the sons of the prophets and of the covenant that God made with your fathers, saying to Abraham, 'And in your offspring shall all the families of the earth be blessed.' God, having raised up his servant, sent him to you first, to bless you by turning every one of you from your wickedness." (3:25–26)

The people of Israel thought of themselves as the fulfillment of God's promise to Abraham, the nation through whom all the families of the earth would be blessed (Gen. 12:3). But Peter says no, this blessing comes through Jesus, the true Israelite. Yes, you had first access to it, but his blessing comes to all who will turn away from the wickedness of rejecting him and toward him in dependence. Peter is saying, you don't get this blessing of Abraham simply by being an offspring of Abraham. You get this blessing by being *in* this one offspring of Abraham, *in Jesus*.

The Response to It

And as they were speaking to the people, the priests and the captain of the temple and the Sadducees came upon them, greatly annoyed because they were teaching the people and proclaiming in Jesus the resurrection from the dead. (4:1–2)

You can almost see the furrowed brows of the priests, whose job it was to teach, coming to see what this teacher outside the temple is saying. You can almost see the curious captain of the temple, whose job it was to keep order in the enormous temple complex, coming to see what is going on with this crowd that is gathering at the Beautiful Gate. And you can almost see the red faces of the Sadducees, who didn't believe in resurrection, as they listen to Peter make the case that the healing of this man is connected to the prophet's promises of a great resurrection of the dead.

Of course, they're all greatly annoyed! What these apostles are teaching represents a seismic shift away from the temple, where they are heavily invested, and toward the very Jesus they acted to snuff out only a few weeks earlier.

Yet here are Peter and John, proclaiming to an enormous crowd gathered at the temple, that Jesus was not, in fact, dead. He was risen from the dead and still very much alive and at work from his throne in heaven. They're saying that all of the end-time blessings promised to God's people—the curse eradicated, evil destroyed, creation renewed, face-to-face relationship with God experienced by all of his people— are *in Jesus,* this living and enthroned Jesus.

It is at this point that we see two very different responses to the case Peter has made.

> And they arrested them and put them in custody until the next day, for it was already evening. But many of those who had heard the word believed, and the number of the men came to about five thousand. (4:3–4)

The response of the priests, temple guards, and Sadducees was essentially: "We'll use our power to put an end to this message about Jesus." As if they could. The response of five thousand of those who heard Peter's explanation of the miracle as evidence for the inauguration of the Old Testament's promises of restoration was: "I want in on this restoration power! I want to be made new! I want the Holy Spirit to come and dwell in me! I want to turn my back on a lifetime of empty religiosity and turn toward the risen and ascended Lord Jesus, believing that as I become joined to him, his resurrection life will go to work in me, believing that the 'perfect healing' that was experienced by that lame man will one day define not only my life but the atmosphere of the whole of creation."

So Peter and John spent the night in custody. And the next day they were called before this religious court. Keep in mind that this is the same court that Jesus stood before only few weeks prior. And we know how that turned out for him. *Same court as Jesus*

> On the next day their rulers and elders and scribes gathered together in Jerusalem, with Annas the high priest and Caiaphas and John and Alexander, and all who were of the high-priestly family. And when they had set them in the midst, they inquired, "By what power or by what name did you do this?" (4:5–7)

I think they already know they've healed the man in the name of Jesus, don't you? Isn't that name the reason these two have been arrested and not merely ignored?

> Then Peter, filled with the Holy Spirit, said to them, "Rulers of the people and elders, if we are being examined today concerning a good deed done to a crippled man, by what means this man has been healed, let it be known to all of you and to all the people of Israel that by the name of Jesus Christ of Nazareth, whom you crucified, whom God raised from the dead—by him this man is standing before you well. This Jesus is the stone that was rejected by you, the builders, which has become the cornerstone." (4:8–11)

Peter pulls out the songbook from which they've all been singing their whole lives and points to Psalm 118. The song speaks of builders who reject a particular stone only to discover that someone has placed that rejected stone in the very foundation of the building. Peter is putting these religious leaders into the song as the builders who rejected the cornerstone, Jesus. He's saying that God himself, by raising Jesus from the dead and seating him at his right hand, has placed Jesus as the foundation stone for the new building, the new people of God, the new temple in which God intends to dwell by his Spirit.

> And there is salvation in no one else, for there is no other name under heaven given among men by which we must be saved." (4:12)

The Greek word used to describe what happened to the lame man back in verse 9, "healed," is the same word used here in verse 12 and translated "saved." To be saved is to experience the healing, wholeness, and all-encompassing restoration that is available only in Jesus Christ.

My friend, your healing begins when you become joined to Jesus by faith so that his resurrection life flows into your life. His resurrection life goes to work in the interior of your life, making you new so that you think new thoughts and feel new feelings so that you begin to desire the things that please him. This is the way he is bringing healing to your life in the here and now. But there is so much more healing ahead. Your healing will come to full fruition on the day of "the resurrection from the dead," when the resurrection life that raised the body of Jesus will raise your body. Jesus, the man of heaven, will return to this earth, and just as that lame man instantly rose, so you will rise from your grave. And it won't only be the bodies of believers that will experience this promised restoration. On that day, Jesus will resurrect, renew, and restore all of creation.

So how did the council Peter and John stood before respond to what they had to say? According to verse 13, the religious leaders were actually very impressed with Peter and John's boldness. Peter and John had not received the same kind of education they had, and yet their ability to connect the dots of the whole of the Old Testament was impressive. The healed man is standing in front of them crediting Peter and John for his healing. But none of that matters. It's all a threat to their deeply entrenched understanding of the way God's plans will be worked out in the world, and it's a threat to their positions in the temple. So they send Peter and John off, charging them to stop talking about Jesus.

It is almost laughable. Clearly that's not going to happen!

> Peter and John answered them, "Whether it is right in the sight of God to listen to you rather than to God, you must judge, for we cannot but speak of what we have seen and heard." (4:19–20)

Jesus had said, "You will be my witnesses." And it's true. The spread of the message of salvation in Jesus Christ can't be stopped. It's going to spread throughout Jerusalem, and then to Judea and Samaria, and then to the ends of the earth. These witnesses are not intimidated, and they're not about to dilute the gospel message. They're emboldened. They're emboldened because they know that they are right at the center of the outworking of God's plans for history.

The Plan That Predestined It

At this point, Peter and John think back to Psalm 2, a song that has shaped them for the whole of their lives, and they recognize the intimidation of the religious leaders for what it is, an outworking of this ongoing conflict. They connect the words of Psalm 2 to the opposition they are experiencing from the religious rulers:

> " 'Why did the Gentiles rage,
>   and the peoples plot in vain?
> The kings of the earth set themselves,
>   and the rulers were gathered together,
>   against the Lord and against his Anointed'—

for truly in this city there were gathered together against your holy servant Jesus, whom you anointed, both Herod and Pontius Pilate, along with the Gentiles and the peoples of Israel, to do whatever your hand and your plan had predestined to take place." (4:25–28)

They don't see this opposition as God's plan spinning out of control but as God's plan falling into place. And they want to be a part of it. No reservations. They're all in. They pray:

"And now, Lord, look upon their threats and grant to your servants to continue to speak your word with all boldness, while you stretch out your hand to heal, and signs and wonders are performed through the name of your holy servant Jesus." And when they had prayed, the place in which they were gathered together was shaken, and they were all filled with the Holy Spirit and continued to speak the word of God with boldness. (4:29–31)

They've been warned to stop talking about Jesus. But they won't stop. It's going to get them killed. But they are bold, not intimidated. They've been empowered by the Spirit to declare the best answer imaginable to the question at the heart of the world's greatest fear: What is this world coming to? Their answer: It is going to be restored and renewed. Not through human effort. Not through political positions or power. Not through social programs. *In Jesus* the resurrection from the dead. Perfect healing by the power of Jesus. Ultimate salvation found only in the name of Jesus.

The same Spirit who filled them with boldness lives in you and can fill you with the same boldness. So let's be bold. Let's be unafraid to declare the name of Jesus. Let's be unwilling to water it down or use euphemisms or more socially acceptable forms.

Recently I saw a clip from a press conference in which members of the University of Oklahoma women's softball team were taking questions about their pursuit of the national championship. When asked how she handles the pressures of the game, Grace Lyons said, "The only way to have a joy that doesn't fade away is from the Lord. . . . Softball can't bring you that."

"We're not afraid to lose," said Jayda Coleman. "We want to win, but it's not the end of the world because our life is in Christ, and that's all that matters."

And then Alyssa Brito: "We're fixing our eyes on Christ. You can't find fulfillment in an outcome, whether it's good or bad. That's why we're so steady in what we do. We know this game is giving us the opportunity to glorify God. . . . Once I turned to Jesus and realized how he had changed my outlook on life, not just softball, but understanding how much I have to live for, and that's living to exemplify the kingdom. That brings so much freedom. . . . This isn't our home. We have so much more. We have an eternity of joy with our Father and I'm excited about that. No matter what, my sisters in Christ will be with me in the end when we're with our king."[1]

They believe it, *in Jesus the resurrection from the dead*. They make me want to be bold. Let's be bold to speak the name of Jesus. Let's proclaim the best answer imaginable to the question, Where is this world headed? We can say, "In Jesus the resurrection from the dead."

---

1   "WCWS Oklahoma Pregame Press Conference," NCAA Championships, YouTube, June 6, 2023, held in Oklahoma City, OK, on June 6, 2023, https://www.youtube.com/.

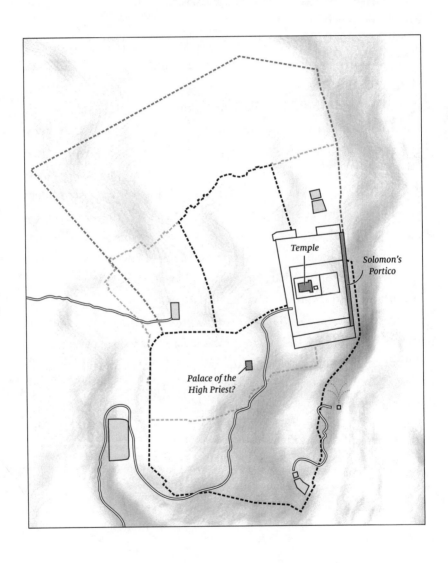

Temple

Solomon's
Portico

*Palace of the
High Priest?*

4

You Will Not Be Able to Overthrow Them

Acts 4:32–5:42

WHEN THINGS ARE FRESH AND NEW and vulnerable, we want to protect them. So when our plants are just beginning to bud, we cover them when the weather report predicts frost. We hold our children's hands to protect them when we cross the street. And we are slow to share our new ideas with people who might shoot them down before they even have the time to fully take shape.

As we come to the end of Acts 4 and work our way through Acts 5, we're peering into the life of the new-covenant community of believers in Christ in its infancy. We know where it is headed. Jesus said, "I will build my church" (Matt. 16:18). The future of this new community is certain because this gospel is unstoppable. But how will Jesus work by his Spirit to protect his infant church from internal and external threats that arise—threats to their unity, their integrity, and their tenacity in proclaiming Christ?

First, let's take stock of where we are. In chapter 2, we saw this church grow by three thousand in one day, and then in chapter 4, it grew by five thousand. This new community is made up of literally thousands of new Christians. Imagine the challenges your church would face if that happened. Now that they've become followers of the Way, which most of their Jewish neighbors think is a heretical sect of the Judaism they love, certainly some of these new believers were losing their jobs and their customers or were being rejected by their families and therefore losing their inheritances. For many of these new believers, suddenly there was no money coming in to pay the bills and to feed their children. But they were regularly meeting with other new believers, some of whom had significant resources.

> Now the full number of those who believed were of one heart and soul, and no one said that any of the things that belonged to him was his own, but they had everything in common. And with great power the apostles were giving their testimony to the resurrection of the Lord Jesus. And great grace was upon them all. There was not a needy person among them, for as many as were owners of lands or houses sold them and brought the proceeds of what was sold and laid it at the apostles' feet, and it was distributed to each as any had need. (4:32–35)

If we're concerned about the threat of disunity due to disparity of their resources, our fears are relieved. Why? Because the Spirit that indwells these new believers has been at work creating a oneness of heart and soul, a pervasive unity across economic barriers so that they are saying, *Whatever is mine is yours. If you have a need that I can meet, I want to meet it.*

Made Unstoppable by Gracious Generosity

The apostles are out there *speaking* of the grace available to all in Jesus, but they're also among their brothers and sisters *experiencing* that grace in significant quantities. This grace is pouring over them and working its

way through them so that it is now flowing out from them in the form
of radical generosity to others in the community whom they may not
have known or been willing to associate with only a few weeks before.
Grace has gone to work so that the things that used to divide them have
no power to do so anymore. They are of one heart and soul because
all of them have become savingly connected to the same Lord Jesus.

An amazing thing is happening. Those who had ownership of land
are putting those plots of land up for sale to raise cash to meet the
needs of others. To take this in, we need to consider what it meant to
own property in the land promised to Abraham, Isaac, and Jacob. To
have land in the promised land was to have a stake in God and all his
promises to bless his people. This is why there were the Old Testament
levirate laws of marriage that kept land in a family (Deut. 25:5–6)
and why land would be returned to its original owners in the year of
jubilee (Lev. 25:28).

But something is becoming clear to these new believers in Jerusalem.
They have a stake in God and all of his promises to bless his people—not
through a deed to a plot of land but by faith in the person of Christ.
All that they stand to inherit by being in Christ is so real to them that
they're finding their grip loosening on what they've inherited from their
earthly family. They want to meet the needs of their new family, the family of those who have put their faith in Christ, if they have the means.

They've become united to Christ in his death and resurrection. The
old self that hoarded money is dead. Died with Christ. And the new
self that seeks to steward wealth for God's glory and the good of others now lives. They want to live out this new resurrection life down to
the penny.

I think we should stop to realize that people in that day had no less
desire for financial security and the benefits of wealth than we do in our
day. Most of us likely approach giving in terms of tithing a percentage
of our income. But how many of us have ever experienced such great
grace that we've been motivated to sell off assets that we were counting

on handing down to our children or supporting us in our old age to meet the needs of brothers and sisters in Christ? The same grace that poured over these early believers has been poured over us. And the same Spirit that dwelt in them dwells in us. Don't we want the grace of God to go to work in us, loosening our grip on money, making us cheerful, generous, gracious givers who find incredible joy in meeting the desperate needs of our brothers and sisters?

Luke wants to focus in on one particular person who sold off land to meet the needs of others, someone we're going to hear about again as we work our way through the book of Acts:

> Thus Joseph, who was also called by the apostles Barnabas (which means son of encouragement), a Levite, a native of Cyprus, sold a field that belonged to him and brought the money and laid it at the apostles' feet. (4:36–37)

Barnabas sold off some of the family land and gave the money to the twelve apostles, no strings attached. How could he do that? Barnabas knows that no matter what, he's not going to lose out (Luke 6:38). He knows that because he is in Christ, he has everything to gain. Indeed, he anticipates inheriting not merely a plot of land in the Middle East but the entire earth (Rom. 4:13).

Made Unstoppable by Spiritual Integrity

Notice the first word in chapter 5: "But." We're about to read the account of a couple that does many of the same things Barnabas did, *but* there is a key difference:

> But a man named Ananias, with his wife Sapphira, sold a piece of property, and with his wife's knowledge he kept back for himself some of the proceeds and brought only a part of it and laid it at the apostles' feet. (5:1–2)

They weren't obligated to sell their property. More than that, they weren't obligated to give *all* of the money from the sale to be distributed to those in need by the disciples. So what's the problem? The problem is their duplicity and hypocrisy that threaten the purity and integrity of the church.

Perhaps they saw how everyone in the community was moved and impressed by the generosity of Barnabas and other landowners, and they wanted that same adulation. Evidently, they wanted a reputation for sacrificial generosity without the sacrifice. They wanted to appear more spiritual, more generous, than they really were. So they presented their gift *as if* they were giving the whole of the proceeds of their sale of land.

> But Peter said, "Ananias, why has Satan filled your heart to lie to the Holy Spirit and to keep back for yourself part of the proceeds of the land? While it remained unsold, did it not remain your own? And after it was sold, was it not at your disposal? Why is it that you have contrived this deed in your heart? You have not lied to man but to God." (5:3–4)

Luke doesn't tell us how Peter knew that Ananias was misrepresenting his gift. But clearly the Holy Spirit was at work making it known to Peter through either extraordinary or ordinary means. It's not just that they lied to the apostles and the entire community. This was God's representative community on earth, so lying to the apostles and the community was lying to God himself.

Peter can see where this deceit finds its true source. In the lying voice of Ananias, Peter recognizes the voice of the father of lies (John 8:44). He says that Satan has filled his heart to do this. Jesus had told his disciples that he would build his church and that the gates of hell will not prevail against it (Matt. 16:18). That would lead one to think that the powers of hell are going to come against it. Satan isn't wasting any time. Satan is at work in this internal threat to the integrity and purity of the new community. But God is also at work to protect and preserve the integrity of this new community.

> When Ananias heard these words, he fell down and breathed his last. And great fear came upon all who heard of it. The young men rose and wrapped him up and carried him out and buried him. (5:5–6)

Suddenly struck dead. Yikes. What do we do with this?

First, we should remember that we've seen this before at several points in the story of God's work among his people when his holiness was disregarded. We think of Nadab and Abihu, who "offered unauthorized fire before the LORD. . . . And fire came out from before the LORD and consumed them" (Lev. 10:1–2). There was Achan, who, after being told to devote to destruction all of the spoils of Jericho, hid a few items in his tent and then lied about it to Joshua and was stoned with stones (Josh. 7). Uzzah put out his hand to the ark of God when the oxen stumbled and was immediately stuck down (2 Sam. 6).

While we are tempted to be shocked at what may seem like harsh judgment from God in these rare situations recorded in the Bible, perhaps we should actually be shocked that it doesn't happen more often! In introducing himself to Moses, God said that he is slow to anger and abundant in mercy (Ex. 34:6). But clearly he is not always slow. I wonder if these instances of instantaneous judgment are there so that we will know that we dare not presume upon his mercy.

I'll never forget something one of my former pastors told me about a conversation he had with an elder who was leaving his wife for another woman. The man said to my pastor, "God will forgive me." And my pastor said in reply, "I wouldn't be so sure." He was putting God to the test. It's a wonder that he didn't die on the spot. If he had, I imagine it would have given pause to a lot of men and women who are tempted to presume upon God's forgiveness and therefore harm the integrity of the church.

> After an interval of about three hours his wife came in, not knowing what had happened. And Peter said to her, "Tell me whether you sold the land for so much." And she said, "Yes, for so much." But Peter said to her, "How is it that you have agreed together to test the Spirit of the Lord? Behold, the feet of those who have buried your husband are at the door, and they will carry you out." Immediately she fell down at his feet and breathed her last. When the young men came in they found her dead, and they carried her out and buried her beside her husband. (5:7–10)

Rather than saying that Sapphira lied to the Holy Spirit, Peter says that she tested the Spirit of the Lord. What does it mean to test the Lord? When the children of Israel complained that God had led them out in the wilderness to allow them to die of thirst, Moses described it as putting the Lord to the test. They were putting his patience with them to the test. When Satan tempted Jesus to throw himself down from the pinnacle of the temple to prove that God would miraculously save him, Jesus answered with Moses's words from Deuteronomy: "You shall not put the Lord your God to the test" (Luke 4:12). So in what way did Ananias and Sapphira put God to the test?

In their deceit, Ananias and Sapphira lied to the Holy Spirit, not merely to test to see if he would know it was a lie. Of course he would. The test was to see if he would tolerate being lied to. The test was to see if God would permit them to get away with appearing more generous, more godly, than they really were. And the answer came swiftly. No, he will not. His judgment is sometimes slow, but it is certain. Nothing gets by him. All sin is dealt with in perfect justice.

We picture the side-by-side graves of Ananias and Sapphira, and we agree with the writer of Hebrews: "It is a fearful thing to fall into the hands of the living God" (Heb. 10:31). That's exactly how it impacted those who witnessed it:

> And great fear came upon the whole church and upon all who heard of these things. (5:11)

This is the healthy fear of the Lord that comes from knowing who he is, what he expects of those who call themselves by his name, and what he is able to do. The whole church must have sensed the gravity of what it means to trifle with a holy God, as the Spirit worked in them to rid them of hypocrisy and develop in them integrity. The Spirit was also at work in them to develop tenacity in the face of intimidation.

Made Unstoppable by Joyful Tenacity

In verse 12 we read that "many signs and wonders were regularly done among the people by the hands of the apostles." It wasn't just people in Jerusalem who were taking note. "People also gathered from the towns around Jerusalem, bringing the sick and those afflicted with unclean spirits, and they were all healed" (5:16). People are no longer bringing their needs to the temple leaders. And the temple leaders don't like it one bit. The people are taking their needs to these bumpkins from Galilee. And what's worse, people are getting healed!

> But the high priest rose up, and all who were with him (that is, the party of the Sadducees), and filled with jealousy they arrested the apostles and put them in the public prison. (5:17–18)

This is the same high priest and council that had been jealous of Jesus. And we know how that turned out.

Amazingly, the members of the council actually think they can stop the spread of the gospel through intimidation. They don't know that it is unstoppable.

> But during the night an angel of the Lord opened the prison doors and brought them out, and said, "Go and stand in the temple and speak to the people all the words of this Life." And when they heard this, they entered the temple at daybreak and began to teach. (5:19–21)

Prison doors are no match for the power of God. The intimidation of a spiritually powerless religious council is no match for the clear instruction of an angel of the Lord. So the angel brings them out, and they go right back to doing exactly what they were arrested for. There is a tenacity to their mission because of their message. They're speaking "all the words of this Life." Notice that "Life" is capitalized. This is the Life that is Christ. Who are these religious leaders to tell the apostles to be silent when an angel of the Lord tells them to speak the very words that bring life to those who are spiritually dead?

The council gets back together the next day and calls for the apostles to be brought before them, only to find out they're no longer in prison; they're back at the temple teaching! How embarrassing.

> Then the captain with the officers went and brought them, but not by force, for they were afraid of being stoned by the people. (5:26)

The council is not giving up on intimidating them into silence, but they're asking politely for the opportunity this time because they fear what will happen if they drag these men away from the people who are leaning in to hear their message and experience their healing. Once the apostles are back in front of the court, the high priest says to them:

"We strictly charged you not to teach in this name, yet here you have filled Jerusalem with your teaching, and you intend to bring this man's blood upon us." (5:28)

This council paid blood money to Judas in their plot to kill Jesus. This council incited the people to say, in calling for Jesus's crucifixion, "His blood be on us and on our children!" (Matt. 27:25). And now they're accusing the apostles of making them responsible for Jesus's death?

But Peter and the apostles answered, "We must obey God rather than men." (5:29)

They can't be silenced. They can't be intimidated into disobeying the clear command of God. Evidently, not only can the council not stop the apostles from speaking the "words of this Life"—the gospel—to the crowds at the temple; they can't stop the apostles from speaking the truth of the gospel to *them*! The council has summoned them and now they have to listen to them. Peter continues:

"The God of our fathers raised Jesus, whom you killed by hanging him on a tree. God exalted him at his right hand as Leader and Savior, to give repentance to Israel and forgiveness of sins. And we are witnesses to these things, and so is the Holy Spirit, whom God has given to those who obey him." (5:30–32)

You killed him; God exalted him. Peter points the finger at them for the death of Jesus. But what is beautiful and amazing is that Peter also holds out grace to them. To the leaders of Israel Peter says, "Jesus can be your leader." To the chief priest who doesn't realize he is facing a future of judgment Peter says, "Jesus can be your Savior." The grace of repentance and forgiveness is available from Jesus to even these religious leaders who killed Jesus. The Holy Spirit will be given to even these hard-hearted religionists, if they will only humble themselves and embrace Jesus as the Christ.

We so wish they would be moved by this grace, humbled by this grace. But sadly, they're not.

When they heard this, they were enraged and wanted to kill them. (5:33)

In the previous chapter we read that the council was "annoyed" when the apostles healed the lame man. Clearly things have now escalated. Now they want to kill these dispensers of grace. There is, however, at least one cool head in the room, someone who has the wisdom of experience. Gamaliel reminds the council of previous troublemakers who seemed to be a huge threat to their power at particular moments in history but eventually died, and those who followed them scattered. Their cause fizzled out. Perhaps this will happen with this whole Jesus thing too. Gamaliel advises the council:

"So in the present case I tell you, keep away from these men and let them alone, for if this plan or this undertaking is of man, it will fail; but if it is of God, you will not be able to overthrow them. You might even be found opposing God!" (5:38–39)

Perhaps Gamaliel senses something different in this band of Galileans. They're doing signs and wonders, and he has heard Peter and the apostles speak on two occasions. Something about them has given him pause. Maybe what they're saying is true. Maybe the Life they are offering is real. He is wise enough to know that nothing can stop the purposes of God.

So they took his advice, and when they had called in the apostles, they beat them and charged them not to speak in the name of Jesus, and let them go. (5:39–40)

This time, the council did not send them off merely with threats. They sent them away bruised and bloodied, and maybe with some broken bones. Because of that, I can think of a number of ways that this chapter might end:

So they went home and nursed their wounds and kept quiet for a while.

So they took some time to reconsider if risking their life for a Messiah they could no longer see with their eyes was going to be worth what it was going to cost them.

So they begged God to exercise the same kind of instantaneous judgment on these cold religious leaders that he had exacted on Ananias and Sapphira.

But instead, we read:

Then they left the presence of the council, rejoicing that they were counted worthy to suffer dishonor for the name. And every day, in the temple and from house to house, they did not cease teaching and preaching that the Christ is Jesus. (5:41–42)

What tenacity in the face of intimidation! They're not depressed about the increased violence against them. They're rejoicing. They're not wondering if speaking of Jesus is going to be worth what it may cost them. They've done the math and are happy to be "counted worthy to suffer dishonor for the name." They're not slowing down; they "did not cease" teaching and preaching. Clearly the Spirit within them has filled them with tenacity to keep on speaking "the words of this Life" in the face of life-threatening intimidation.

As we take in their tenacity in the face of life-threatening intimidation, it leads me to ask myself and you, my reader—has something or someone intimidated us into backing down from speaking "the words of this Life"? Are we afraid of losing our jobs, afraid of no longer getting invited, afraid of being canceled as religious nuts? If so, there is a joy we are missing out on. We're missing out on the joy of being counted worthy to suffer dishonor for the name of Jesus Christ. Seeing their tenacity makes us want to ask the Spirit to fill us with this same kind of tenacity, this same kind of courage, and this same kind of joy, doesn't it?

As we saw the boldness of the apostles in chapters 3 and 4, we were challenged to be bold in our witness. In 4:32–5:42, I think the challenge for us is to be generous with our brothers and sisters instead of stingy. It is to be sincere rather than hypocritical, and to be joyfully tenacious in sharing the word of Life rather than fearfully silent.

We can be sure that just as the Holy Spirit provided what was needed to meet every threat that arose in the life of this infant church—threats to their unity, their integrity, and their tenacity in proclaiming Christ—he will also empower us to withstand threats to our unity, our integrity, and our tenacity in proclaiming Christ. We can be generous in giving toward the needs of others, knowing that everything we give will be invested for us in heaven. Every time we are tempted to appear more spiritual and sacrificial than we really are, we can resist, knowing that we will not regret forgoing glory now for the eternal glory to come. And every time we suffer dishonor for the name now, we can be sure that there is profound joy for us in it now, and unending joy when he comes.

Mediterranean Sea

CANAAN

Shechem•
◇Jerusalem

•Haran

MESOPOTAMIA

Ur •

EGYPT

SINAI

MIDIAN

▲ Mount Sinai?

Red Sea

5

The Most High Does Not Dwell
in Houses Made by Hands

Acts 6:1–7:60

WHEN I WAS GROWING UP, if I wanted to communicate with someone in another city or country but didn't want to pay an enormous long-distance telephone bill, I had to write or type out a letter, find the right stamp, and send it in the mail. It might be days before the letter was received. If I wanted to find the phone number for a business, I had to pull out the yellow pages, find the right category, and look up the number. If I wanted to figure out how to get somewhere, I had to unfold and then figure out how to refold a map. If I wanted a picture of something, I needed a camera, and then I had to drop off the film and wait days for the pictures to be developed.

Then in 1971 a guy named Ray Tomlinson sent the first email. The first mobile phone with internet access was launched in Finland in 1996, and then on June 29, 2007 the first iPhone went on sale. It's fair to say that these developments created a seismic shift in the way we communicate with each other. We can send messages instantly. We no longer need yellow pages, or sets of encyclopedias, or film, or fold-up maps. Everything we need is on this device that over seven billion of us carry around. Our smartphones have made all these other things obsolete.

In the book of Acts, something similar is happening. The old ways of life centered around the temple in Jerusalem are becoming obsolete. For centuries Jewish people had built their whole lives around the temple— around its sacrifices and ceremony, around its laws and its leadership. But then, around AD 30 something began to shift. A carpenter from Nazareth began to teach and preach. He had the gall to say to a group of Pharisees, the most respected of the religious leaders, "Something *greater* than the temple is here." And he was talking about himself! They ended up crucifying him for it. But he didn't stay dead. After his resurrection and ascension, he sent the Holy Spirit to dwell, not in the Most Holy Place of the temple in Jerusalem, but within those who had put their faith in him. What the temple in Jerusalem had always provided was now available in and through Jesus.

We've seen in these first few chapters of Acts that this seismic shift in how a person finds acceptance before God and a home among God's people has created increasing animosity between the followers of Jesus and the temple authorities. First, the apostles were arrested and released. But they didn't back down on speaking about Christ. Then they were arrested and beaten and released. Again, they were not intimidated into silence. In the scene we're coming to in Acts 6 and 7, we're going to see the conflict created by this seismic shift away from the temple in Jerusalem and toward faith in Jesus Christ come to a murderous climax.

But first we must be introduced to the person at the center of the conflict in these chapters—Stephen.

Stephen's Service

Notice, in particular, the words Luke uses to describe the character and ministry of Stephen.

Now in these days when the disciples were increasing in number, a complaint by the Hellenists arose against the Hebrews because their widows were being neglected in the daily distribution. (6:1)

Who were the Hellenists? The Hellenists were Jews who had lived outside of Palestine at some point and therefore spoke Greek. At this point in Acts, they're living in Jerusalem where the dominant languages are Hebrew and Aramaic. Greek-, Aramaic-, and Hebrew-speaking believers have become brothers and sisters in the church. But there's a problem. A language barrier, and perhaps a cultural barrier, has caused a breakdown that means the Greek-speaking widows in the church are not getting the daily distribution of food they need, while evidently the Aramaic-speaking widows are being taken care of. Something needs to be done.[1]

And the twelve summoned the full number of the disciples and said, "It is not right that we should give up preaching the word of God to serve tables. Therefore, brothers, pick out from among you seven men of good repute, full of the Spirit and of wisdom, whom we will appoint to this duty. But we will devote ourselves to prayer and to the ministry of the word." And what they said pleased the whole gathering, and they chose Stephen, a man full of faith and of the Holy Spirit, and Philip, and Prochorus, and Nicanor, and Timon, and Parmenas, and Nicolaus, a proselyte of Antioch. These they set before the apostles, and they prayed and laid their hands on them. (6:2–6)

Evidently the Greek-speaking brothers in the church were told to pick out seven men among them who would do right by these widows. One of the men chosen was Stephen, who was "a man full of faith and of the Holy Spirit."

---

1   This paragraph and several others in this chapter are adapted from Nancy Guthrie, *Saints and Scoundrels in the Story of Jesus* (Wheaton, IL: Crossway, 2019), 172–77, 181–83. Used by permission.

And the word of God continued to increase, and the number of the disciples multiplied greatly in Jerusalem, and a great many of the priests became obedient to the faith. (6:7)

Luke has paused the story to give us a little snapshot of how things are going in the "you shall be my witnesses" department. The apostles and the rest of the Jesus followers are witnessing to the resurrection of Jesus, and their numbers are multiplying day by day. Amazingly many priests were becoming a part of the church. (Perhaps it shouldn't be so amazing since priests should have known the Scriptures and therefore been able to recognize that Jesus was the Christ.) Imagine how angry these "defections" of so many people, including many of the priests, would have made the temple leaders.

And then there's something else going on that is stoking their anger.

And Stephen, full of grace and power, was doing great wonders and signs among the people. (6:8)

The priests are defecting, and the people are transferring their allegiance from religious authorities who have no grace and no power to this new-covenant community where they're finding healing and wholeness in spirit and body. We probably shouldn't be surprised that the religious leaders decide to take action against what they see as competition for the people's allegiance.

Stephen Seized

Then some of those who belonged to the synagogue of the Freedmen (as it was called), and of the Cyrenians, and of the Alexandrians, and of those from Cilicia and Asia, rose up and disputed with Stephen. (6:9)

There was only one temple, which was in Jerusalem, but evidently there were numerous synagogues in population centers around the known world where Jews had settled. Synagogues were at the center of Jewish life. They were gathering places where Jews came together to read and discuss the Torah. What was the synagogue of Freedmen? Freedmen were former slaves or the children of former slaves who had been emancipated by their owners. Perhaps this was the synagogue that Stephen had attended before he came to faith in Christ and was still attending to engage with the Greek-speaking Jews there about Jesus Christ. Perhaps when Stephen took his turn to speak at the synagogue he was saying things like, "Now that the once-for-all perfect sacrifice has been offered, we don't need to be taking sacrifices to the temple anymore. In fact, we don't even need the temple building anymore. Jesus is the only temple we need."

> But they could not withstand the wisdom and the Spirit with which he was speaking. Then they secretly instigated men who said, "We have heard him speak blasphemous words against Moses and God." And they stirred up the people and the elders and the scribes, and they came upon him and seized him and brought him before the council. (6:10–12)

Evidently those who gathered in the Freedmen's synagogue became increasingly angry. Likely these are people who have come to live in Jerusalem because they wanted to be near the temple. It was everything to them. So they really didn't appreciate Stephen suggesting that it was no longer needed. But they didn't know how to argue with Stephen because he supported everything he said with their own Scriptures. He spoke with so much wisdom and spiritual power. So what did they do? They rounded up some people who were willing to offer false testimony against Stephen before the religious council.

> And they set up false witnesses who said, "This man never ceases to speak words against this holy place and the law, for we have heard

him say that this Jesus of Nazareth will destroy this place and will change the customs that Moses delivered to us." (6:13–14)

Can you hear the echoes of the accusations made against Jesus before this same council? Remember how false witnesses twisted Jesus's words, "Destroy this temple, and in three days I will raise it up" (John 2:19), and falsely accused him of threatening to tear down the temple? Notice carefully the two accusations: he's threatening to destroy the temple, and he's seeking to change the law of Moses.

And gazing at him, all who sat in the council saw that his face was like the face of an angel. (6:15)

This is interesting. It must have been maddening to the council that just as they were accusing Stephen of showing disrespect for the law of Moses, his face began to glow in the same way Moses's face had glowed when he came down the mountain after receiving the law written on stone! Perhaps that should have been a sign that Stephen had a better grasp on the law of Moses than they did.

And the high priest said, "Are these things so?" (7:1)

We hear the head of the Sanhedrin, the high priest, Caiaphas, the same high priest Jesus had stood before only weeks earlier, ask Stephen if what they were saying about him was true. We might hope Stephen would answer softly to stay out of trouble or come up with something that would clear his name. But that's not what he does. Instead, he launches into a Bible overview, a theological geography lesson, knowing that they're not going to like where the story ends. His central message is that they shouldn't be surprised that the temple in Jerusalem is no longer the place where God meets with his people since God has never been confined to the temple in Jerusalem.

Stephen Speaks

Stephen began his history lesson with the man who stood at the beginning of their history as a people: Abraham. "The God of glory appeared to our father Abraham when he was in Mesopotamia, before he lived in Haran" (7:2). If you look at a map and find the city of Ur, where Abraham lived when God appeared to him, you'll see that it is about 700 miles east of Jerusalem. Stephen wants them to see that long before there was a temple in Jerusalem, the glory of God was in Mesopotamia, appearing to Abraham.

Then he moves on to Joseph. "And the patriarchs, jealous of Joseph, sold him into Egypt; but God was with him" (7:9). In Joseph's day, the glory of God was in Egypt. Egypt is a long way from Jerusalem.

Then Stephen moves on to Moses. Moses was in the wilderness of Mount Sinai when he saw a flame of fire in a bush.

> "When Moses saw it, he was amazed at the sight, and as he drew near to look, there came the voice of the Lord: 'I am the God of your fathers, the God of Abraham and of Isaac and of Jacob.' And Moses trembled and did not dare to look. Then the Lord said to him, 'Take off the sandals from your feet, for the place where you are standing is holy ground.'" (7:31–33)

Long before there was a temple in Jerusalem, the glory of God was in the west side of the Sinai wilderness, speaking to Moses, declaring the dusty ground Moses was standing on to be holy because of his presence there.

Later, after leading the Israelites out of Egypt, Moses was at Mount Sinai. Luke writes that Moses "received living oracles" (7:38) from God there on the mountain. And how did the people respond to the law that was given to them?

"Our fathers refused to obey him, but thrust him aside, and in their hearts they turned to Egypt, saying to Aaron, 'Make for us gods who will go before us. As for this Moses who led us out from the land of Egypt, we do not know what has become of him.' And they made a calf in those days, and offered a sacrifice to the idol and were rejoicing in the works of their hands." (7:39–41)

Stephen has just been accused of mishandling the law of Moses, so in his history lesson he points out how the people of Israel have responded to the law of Moses from the get-go. They've rejected it for idolatry. And notice who is at the center of this rejection of the law: Aaron, the first high priest. This reminder of the first high priest and the way he led the nation of Israel into idolatry was a pointed indictment of the high priest and the leadership Stephen was addressing. Rather than making a golden calf to worship as an idol like Aaron did, these men have turned the temple itself into an idol to worship.

Stephen then moves on to the "tent of witness" or tabernacle in which God came down to dwell among his people in the wilderness. Long before there was a temple in Jerusalem, God dwelt among his people in the Most Holy Place of the tabernacle that moved from place to place in the wilderness. Later it was with them in the land of promise, Canaan, going with them wherever they went. Finally Stephen gets to the temple in Jerusalem built by Solomon. And perhaps the council is just about to say, "Aha! See? The temple was then and remains now the place where God dwells among his people!" But before they can offer that argument, Stephen refutes it. First, he quotes Solomon—the very person who built the temple—saying,

"Yet the Most High does not dwell in houses made by hands." (7:48)

Then he continues quoting the prophet Isaiah:

"As the prophet says,

> 'Heaven is my throne,
>> and the earth is my footstool.
> What kind of house will you build for me, says the Lord,
>> or what is the place of my rest?
> Did not my hand make all these things?'" (Acts 7:48–50;
>> cf. Isa. 66:1–2)

Did you catch that Stephen was hinting that they'd made the temple into an idol? Back in verse 41, when he was talking about the people of Israel making the golden calf, he said they "were rejoicing in the works of their hands." Then here, in verse 48, Stephen says that God does not live in "houses made by hands," referring to the temple in Jerusalem built by human hands. Just as the Israelites in the wilderness made an idol to worship, Stephen suggests that the temple has become an idol that the Jews in his day worship.

By working his way through this theological geography lesson, Stephen clearly demonstrated that the glory of God had never been confined to a temple in Jerusalem. So why were these religious leaders unwilling to accept that God's presence had, in their day, shifted away from the temple in Jerusalem?

Surely part of their resistance was that if they were to accept God's dwelling in his people by his Spirit, it would mean that people no longer needed to come to the temple for access to God. They would lose all their power, position, and purpose for existence.

More significantly, at the heart of their resistance was a misunderstanding of what the temple was always meant to be. The blueprints God gave David for the temple were given as a miniature model of a greater reality, a greater temple, a greater way in which God would one day dwell with his people. Over time, however, the people became wedded to the model and had simply stopped looking for the greater reality that was still to come.

Among my grown son's old toys that are still at our house, there is a little model car. Imagine if we had given Matt this model car when he was twelve or thirteen and told him, "When you're sixteen, we're going to give you a real car. We're giving you this model to help you anticipate that greater gift." Then imagine that when he turned sixteen, we handed him the keys to a brand- new car, and his response was, "No thanks. I don't want that car; I have this model car."

We would have said, "No, Matt, you don't understand. That was always just a model of something far greater that we intended to give you."

And he would get upset and say, "Why do you want to take away my car? Don't you know how important this car is to me?"

That sounds crazy, right? But this was the situation with these religious leaders and the temple. The temple was merely a model of something greater that God intended to give to his people in the person and work of Jesus. But they demanded to hold on to the model. They held on to the shadow and rejected the substance that cast the shadow.

At this point, we realize there is something else feeding their resistance to Stephen's message, a long-standing history of murderous resistance to those who speak for God.

> "You stiff-necked people, uncircumcised in heart and ears, you always resist the Holy Spirit. As your fathers did, so do you." (7:51)

Stephen says that these religious leaders are like a stiff-necked cow that resists the goad of the farmer. In fact, the people of Israel had been this way throughout their history (Ex. 33:3; Deut. 9:13; Neh. 9:16). They stubbornly resisted God at nearly every turn, even as they called themselves by his name. By calling them "uncircumcised in heart and ears," he's saying that though they may have undergone physical circumcision to mark themselves as belonging to God, their hearts are far from him. They refuse to listen to him. They are now refusing to listen to his witnesses.

Which of the prophets did your fathers not persecute? And they killed those who announced beforehand the coming of the Righteous One, whom you have now betrayed and murdered, you who received the law as delivered by angels and did not keep it. (7:52–53)

Throughout Israel's history, they had frequently responded with violence against those who spoke God's word to them. Joseph's brothers (who became the leaders of the twelve tribes) sought to kill Joseph when he prophesied about the future. The Israelites rejected Moses when he took action to deliver them. They rejected and killed many of the prophets who spoke to them about the greater prophet to come. According to tradition, Isaiah was sawn in two.[2] Jeremiah was stoned.[3] Zechariah was stoned in the temple courts (2 Chron. 24:20–21). And then they killed the ultimate prophet, Jesus. Surely even as Stephen spoke to the council so pointedly, he didn't assume that he would be treated any differently. And if so, he was right.

Stephen Is Stoned

Now when they heard these things they were enraged, and they ground their teeth at him. But he, full of the Holy Spirit, gazed into heaven and saw the glory of God, and Jesus standing at the right hand of God. And he said, "Behold, I see the heavens opened, and the Son of Man standing at the right hand of God." (7:54–56)

Stephen's speech had explored where the glory of God had been manifested throughout the history of God's people—in Mesopotamia, in the wilderness, in Egypt. He'd quoted Isaiah 66 about God's throne in heaven. And then heaven opened! Stephen could see the glory of God

2   Ancient Jewish-Christian tradition suggests that Isaiah was martyred by King Manasseh, son of Hezekiah.

3   According to the early church father Tertullian, the Jews stoned Jeremiah to death in Egypt. Jeremiah's "crime" was telling them truths they did not want to hear. *Scorpiace* 8.

with his own eyes! In essence he concluded his history lesson by giving them an update on where the glory of God is now. It isn't in the temple in Jerusalem. It's in heaven where Jesus stands at the right hand of God.

> But they cried out with a loud voice and stopped their ears and rushed together at him. Then they cast him out of the city and stoned him. And the witnesses laid down their garments at the feet of a young man named Saul. And as they were stoning Stephen, he called out, "Lord Jesus, receive my spirit." And falling to his knees he cried out with a loud voice, "Lord, do not hold this sin against them." And when he had said this, he fell asleep. (7:57–60)

"Lord Jesus, receive my spirit," he prayed. Stephen, the man who was described as "full of faith," shows us how a person who is full of faith dies: confident in what Jesus has promised, confident that to be away from the body and at home with the Lord is what awaits all who are savingly connected to Christ. "Lord, do not hold this sin against them" was his other prayer. In contrast to the angry rage that came down on him, even as they were hurling stones at him, Stephen was praying that God would show his murderers mercy.

It is interesting that Luke does not write that Stephen died. Luke chooses to describe the death of Stephen in terms of falling asleep. I think he wants us to see the peacefulness of Stephen even as rage is literally being hurled at him. He's facing death with a restful confidence that neither death nor life will be able to separate him from the love of God in Christ Jesus his Lord (Rom. 8:39). And I think he's communicating that for the person who dies anticipating entering into the glory of Jesus, death is not the end. It is more like falling asleep, awaiting the resurrection morning wake-up call of the Master.

So what do we take away from the example of Stephen, the argument Stephen made, and the death of Stephen? One thing we take away is that what Jesus said is true. "If the world hates you, know that it has hated me before it hated you" (John 15:18). When we point out the idols in people's lives, perhaps especially idols that have given them a sense of religious power and superiority, we shouldn't be surprised when people respond with hatred, throwing everything they can at us to get us to shut up. Stephen's story assures us that we endure harsh words and worse in good company.

While we are not clinging to a temple building in Jerusalem with all its rules and requirements, perhaps we need the theological geography lesson as much as the Sanhedrin did. If we opened up a map of the world, seeking to trace the location of the glory of God, where would we see it today? We'd see a dim glow or just a few dots in places of the world where believers are few, and blinding light where the fellowship of believers is strong. And hopefully we would smile, filled with joy over God's worldwide salvation plan and the spread of his presence indwelling his people first in Jerusalem, then in Judea and Samaria, and now to the ends of the earth, all the way to where we are. I also wonder, if we could see it on a map, if it might prompt us to consider going to where the light of his presence is spotty and dim rather than linger where it is strong.

The good news Stephen shared with the people of his day, and with us, is that you and I don't have to make a trek to any holy place to commune with God, to find forgiveness, to find grace and mercy in our time of need. The Most High does not dwell in houses made by hands. In grace, the Holy Spirit has come to dwell in us, to seal us to Christ, and to lead us into truth. He is at work now transforming us from glory to glory until the day that we, like Stephen, will enter into glory.

PART 2

SALVATION TO JUDEA
AND SAMARIA

Sea of
Galilee

• Caesarea

Mediterranean Sea

SAMARIA

Jordan
River

◇ Jerusalem

•Azotus

JUDEA

• Gaza

Dead
Sea

TO ETHIOPIA

6

They Were All Scattered

Acts 8:1–40

"YOU'RE A GATHERER, AREN'T YOU?"

That's what my friend Courtney Doctor said to me a couple of weeks ago when David and I picked her up to ride with us to an event in Gulf Shores, Alabama, where those working on the event were staying together in a big house.

"Tell me about all of the people who will be in the house," Courtney said. And I proceeded to tell her about each of them—from my cousin who has known me all my life, to some with whom I've shared decades-long friendships, and some I barely knew. We had a fabulous week together leading the conference, enjoying sunshine and sunsets, good meals, meaningful conversations, singing around the piano, and lots of laughter. I must say, I gathered a fine group of people.

I'd like to think that there is something Jesus-like in my love of gathering people. Jesus is a gatherer—actually the greatest of gatherers. Indeed, it was always expected that the Messiah would be a gatherer, gathering up the people of God who had been scattered throughout the known world. Thirteen times the prophet Ezekiel promised that when God's King came, he would gather his people from where they had been scattered. He described the ten northern tribes who had been scattered throughout the nations by Assyria as the "stick of Joseph" and the two southern tribes that had been scattered into exile in Babylon as the "stick of Judah," writing:

> Thus says the Lord GOD: Behold, I am about to take the stick of Joseph (that is in the hand of Ephraim) and the tribes of Israel associated with him. And I will join with it the stick of Judah, and make them one stick, that they may be one in my hand. . . . And one king shall be king over them all, and they shall be no longer two nations, and no longer divided into two kingdoms. (Ezek. 37:19, 22)

The King who would be king over all of them came into this world in the person of Jesus. And from the start of his public ministry, Jesus began to gather people to himself, into his kingdom, under his kingship. On the shores of Galilee, he called four fishmen to leave their nets and begin fishing for people to be gathered to him. But as he went along, it became obvious that the religious establishment didn't approve of those Jesus sought to gather. He gathered tax collectors and notorious sinners, people who were considered unclean and unwelcome. And the religious leaders despised him for it, refusing to be gathered in with those they looked down on. Their resistance caused Jesus to weep over the city, saying, "O Jerusalem, Jerusalem, the city that kills the prophets and stones those who are sent to it! How often would I have gathered your children together as a hen gathers her brood under her wings, and you were not willing!" (Luke 13:34).

But the gathering purposes of Jesus were not thwarted by rejection and unbelief. As he anticipated the cross, Jesus said, "And I, when I am lifted up from the earth, will draw all people to myself" (John 12:32). In his death, resurrection, and ascension, Jesus was lifted up and began drawing people to himself. Then came Pentecost. When the people asked what it meant, Peter told them the promise of forgiveness and the Holy Spirit is for "all who are far off—for all whom the Lord our God will call" (Acts 2:39).

Pentecost marked the beginning of the gathering in of the harvest of God's people to be, as Jesus said, "one flock" under "one shepherd" (John 10:16).

As we come to Acts 8, what we read doesn't initially look much like gathering. It looks like scattering. In the previous chapter we read about the stoning of Stephen, which unleashed a vicious assault on the believers in Jerusalem so that they began to scatter.

> And there arose on that day a great persecution against the church in Jerusalem, and they were all scattered throughout the regions of Judea and Samaria, except the apostles. (8:1)

Jesus had said to his disciples in the upper room, "They will put you out of the synagogues. Indeed, the hour is coming when whoever kills you will think he is offering service to God" (John 16:2). That is exactly how those who were persecuting followers of the Way thought of themselves and their cruelty. Evidently the persecution became intolerable for many of these new believers to continue to live in Jerusalem, and they began to scatter.

The Gathering of Despised Outsiders

Evidently one of those who scattered was Philip, whom we met earlier in Acts 6 when he was chosen as one of the seven men "of good repute, full of the Spirit and of wisdom" appointed to make sure the needs of Greek-speaking widows in the Jerusalem church were not being overlooked. But when we meet Philip again here in chapter 8, he is on a gathering mission.

> Now those who were scattered went about preaching the word. Philip went down to the city of Samaria and proclaimed to them the Christ. (8:4–5)

Philip was headed north toward the capital city of the region of Samaria, which in his day had been renamed Sebaste. Perhaps Luke calls the city "Samaria" because he wants us to think of this city as symbolic of the entire northern kingdom. Samaria represents the descendants of the ten northern tribes who had separated themselves from the two southern tribes a thousand years before. When they were conquered by Assyria in 721 BC, the Assyrians brought people from many of the other nations they had conquered into the territory of the northern kingdom and settled them there. The people of the ten tribes intermarried with those settled from other nations and thereby lost their distinctiveness as descendants of Abraham. This meant that they weren't Jews, but they weren't quite pagan Gentiles either.

It would be an understatement to say that Jews looked down on Samaritans. We get a glimpse of the attitude Jews had toward Samaritans in Luke's Gospel account of what James and John said to Jesus when some Samaritans rejected him: "Lord do you want us to tell fire to come down from heaven and consume them?" (Luke 9:54). "How about we just burn them up!" seems like an extreme response doesn't it? This instinctual response reveals deep-seated derision.

Philip taking the gospel to Samaria was clearly a geographical milestone in the expansion of the kingdom of God and the church's witness. But more than mere geography was being overcome. The deep chasm of religious hostility and exclusion that had separated Jews and Samaritans for generations was being bridged.

And the crowds with one accord paid attention to what was being said by Philip, when they heard him and saw the signs that he did. For unclean spirits, crying out with a loud voice, came out of many who had them, and many who were paralyzed or lame were healed. So there was much joy in that city. (8:6–8)

Imagine what it was like in this city as people who had never been able to walk began to walk, and those who had been inhabited by demons that drove them to do despicable things were freed from that evil. Luke tells us the city lit up with joy.

> But there was a man named Simon, who had previously practiced magic in the city and amazed the people of Samaria, saying that he himself was somebody great. They all paid attention to him, from the least to the greatest, saying, "This man is the power of God that is called Great." And they paid attention to him because for a long time he had amazed them with his magic. But when they believed Philip as he preached good news about the kingdom of God and the name of Jesus Christ, they were baptized, both men and women. Even Simon himself believed, and after being baptized he continued with Philip. And seeing signs and great miracles performed, he was amazed. (8:9–13)

Here is a Samaritan who has made a name for himself and thoroughly enriched himself through the practice of magic empowered by Satan. The people in Samaria seem to think that Simon's power is from God, and he hasn't discouraged them from that notion. But then the people in this city are exposed to the real deal—signs and wonders truly empowered by God. They want this true and real power in their lives. They have paid attention to Simon for a long time. Indeed, Satan has had his run of the place. But a superior power has arrived. The word is being spoken, and it is having its intended effect. Philip is giving out the good news about the kingdom of God and the name of Jesus Christ. Men and women who have always been despised outsiders are being gathered in!

But Philip is not out to start something separate in Samaria from what is happening in Jerusalem. There is to be no separate Samaritan Christianity as there had been a separate Samaritan Judaism. The "stick of Joseph," these despised Samaritan outsiders, must become joined to the "stick of Judah." This means that these new believers in Samaria must become connected to the new believers in Jerusalem. How will that happen?

> Now when the apostles at Jerusalem heard that Samaria had received the word of God, they sent to them Peter and John, who came down and prayed for them that they might receive the Holy Spirit, for he had not yet fallen on any of them, but they had only been baptized in the name of the Lord Jesus. Then they laid their hands on them and they received the Holy Spirit. (8:14–17)

In a sense, this was the Samaritan Pentecost. The believing Samaritans were filled with the same Spirit that filled the believers in Jerusalem. This was proof positive that Jesus had gathered these despised outsiders into the fold along with them. The Samaritans would be counted as full members of the one true church, the new-covenant community of God's people.

The Exclusion of an Unrepentant Profiteer

One thing we know about the covenant community of God's people throughout the ages is that there have always been those who appear to be part of the covenant community but are really out to use God to enrich themselves (think Achan, Judas, Ananias, and Sapphira). And evidently that is the case here in Samaria.

> Now when Simon saw that the Spirit was given through the laying on of the apostles' hands, he offered them money, saying, "Give me this power also, so that anyone on whom I lay my hands may receive the Holy Spirit." (8:18–19)

We're not told what outward manifestation there was when the Samaritans received the Holy Spirit, but it must have been something supernatural for it to appeal to Simon the magician. And though we were told earlier that Simon believed the gospel and was baptized, we begin to wonder if he has truly repented of his old ways of claiming special powers from God as a way to accumulate followers and make money.

> But Peter said to him, "May your silver perish with you, because you thought you could obtain the gift of God with money! You have neither part nor lot in this matter, for your heart is not right before God. Repent, therefore, of this wickedness of yours, and pray to the Lord that, if possible, the intent of your heart may be forgiven you. For I see that you are in the gall of bitterness and in the bond of iniquity." (8:20–23)

Evidently Simon sees the impact of the Spirit on these new Samaritan believers as a money-making opportunity. We may want to believe that Simon's newfound faith is sincere and that he simply wants to be an extension of the ministry of the apostles, but by Peter's response to him, we recognize that a more sinister motive seems to be at work. Notice Peter seems to indicate that Simon will "perish" and that he has "neither part nor lot" in the things of the Spirit. Simon doesn't act like a believer, and Peter speaks to him as if he is not a believer. If he will not repent, there is no place for him in the people of God. He will remain an outsider for all eternity.

> And Simon answered, "Pray for me to the Lord, that nothing of what you have said may come upon me." (8:24)

Is this repentance? Notice that Simon doesn't pray himself. Perhaps he is asking Peter to pull some strings with God so that he will be delivered from the judgment he deserves apart from genuine repentance. Perhaps he is far more interested in avoiding the consequences of his sin than in forsaking his sin. The narrative ends on an unresolved note. Perhaps Luke leaves us hanging a bit so that we will examine ourselves rather than simply focus on Simon. Perhaps we're meant to ask ourselves, "Has the power of the gospel gone to work in me so that repentance has become my modus operandi, especially when I am shown a way that I'm really more interested in using Jesus for my own ends rather than loving and serving Jesus because he is worthy of my devotion?"

> Now when they had testified and spoken the word of the Lord, they returned to Jerusalem, preaching the gospel to many villages of the Samaritans. (8:25)

Samaritans have been welcomed in as full members of the covenant community. That means the apostles simply couldn't make a beeline for Jerusalem, ignoring all the Samaritans living in darkness along the way. Instead, they went from village to village giving out the good news that Jesus was building his kingdom, gathering one flock under one shepherd, a new community made up of Jews and Samaritans and Gentiles. Imagine the surprise in these villages. Jews from Jerusalem were not only making a point to engage with them; they were sharing with them a vision of a new community in which they, as outsiders, were welcomed in.

The Gathering In of Unwelcomed Outcasts

Philip left Jerusalem to gather outsiders into the new-covenant community. But that's not all. He also welcomed in outcasts.

> Now an angel of the Lord said to Philip, "Rise and go toward the south to the road that goes down from Jerusalem to Gaza." This is a desert place. And he rose and went. And there was an Ethiopian, a eunuch, a court official of Candace, queen of the Ethiopians, who was in charge of all her treasure. (8:26–27)

When we read that this man is an Ethiopian, rather than think of him as coming from the modern nation of Ethiopia, we should think of him coming from the nation that is called "Cush" numerous places in the Old Testament (Ps. 68:31; Isa. 11:11; Zeph. 3:9–10). This was the territory just below Egypt, along the Nile River, which is located in the modern nation of Sudan. At the time Acts was written, this was at the boundaries of the known world.[1]

We're told that this man is a court official of Candace, the queen of the Ethiopians. But it doesn't seem to be official business that brought him to Jerusalem.

> He had come to Jerusalem to worship and was returning, seated in his chariot, and he was reading the prophet Isaiah. (8:27–28)

He seems to be on a personal quest. Perhaps he had heard about the God of Israel and how he dwelt in the temple in Jerusalem, and the court official had made the long journey to Jerusalem, only to discover that he couldn't gain entrance to the temple. Not only is he a Gentile; he's a eunuch. And the law given at Mount Sinai had made it clear that "no one whose testicles are crushed or whose male organ is cut off shall enter the assembly of the LORD" (Deut. 23:1).

But he has hope. He has his own copy of the scroll of Isaiah. And the prophet Isaiah has a word of hope for outcasts like him. Here's what Isaiah wrote in Isaiah 56:

> Let not the foreigner who has joined himself to the LORD say,
>   "The LORD will surely separate me from his people";
> and let not the eunuch say,
>   "Behold, I am a dry tree."
> For thus says the LORD:

---

1   Guy Prentiss Waters, *A Study Commentary on the Acts of the Apostles* (Leyland, UK: Evangelical Press, 2015), 215–16.

"To the eunuchs who keep my Sabbaths,
  who choose the things that please me
  and hold fast my covenant,
I will give in my house and within my walls
  a monument and a name
  better than sons and daughters;
I will give them an everlasting name
  that shall not be cut off. . . ."

The Lord GOD,
  who gathers the outcasts of Israel, declares,
"I will gather yet others to him
  besides those already gathered." (Isa. 56:3–5, 8)

Isaiah wrote that there would be a day when foreigners (according to Isaiah 11:11, specifically Cushites) and eunuchs would receive an eternal inheritance and place in the community of God's people. This Ethiopian eunuch may not have known it yet, but that day had come. The temple in Jerusalem had become obsolete in the death and resurrection of Jesus, and with it so had the exclusionary ordinance of forbidding eunuchs into the assembly. Holiness was no longer a matter of externals such as diet or racial decent or physical fitness. It was now solely a matter of being joined to Jesus Christ by faith. God is gathering outcasts to himself.

And the Spirit said to Philip, "Go over and join this chariot." So Philip ran to him and heard him reading Isaiah the prophet and asked, "Do you understand what you are reading?" And he said, "How can I, unless someone guides me?" And he invited Philip to come up and sit with him. Now the passage of the Scripture that he was reading was this:

"Like a sheep he was led to the slaughter
  and like a lamb before its shearer is silent,

so he opens not his mouth.
In his humiliation justice was denied him.
    Who can describe his generation?
For his life is taken away from the earth." (8:29–33; cf.
        Isa. 53:7–8)

With his Isaiah scroll open, he just happens to be reading a passage that is clearly about Jesus, out loud, when Philip comes upon him. He asks for help in understanding it (every aspiring evangelist's dream). God is at work sovereignly overseeing the gathering of former outcasts into becoming full participants in his holy community.

And the eunuch said to Philip, "About whom, I ask you, does the prophet say this, about himself or about someone else?" Then Philip opened his mouth, and beginning with this Scripture he told him the good news about Jesus. (8:34–35)

Wouldn't you have loved to hear how Philip articulated the good news about Jesus from Isaiah 53? Maybe he said something like this:

This passage is about the suffering servant, Jesus of Nazareth, who was crucified just a short time ago in Jerusalem. He was despised and rejected, like you were in Jerusalem. The world saw his death as a great humiliation, but it was really his great exaltation. The world saw only agony and defeat, but it accomplished a glorious victory. Indeed, God was at work in his death and resurrection to accomplish his good purposes for people like me and you. According to Isaiah, God says that through the death of "the righteous one, my servant," many will be "accounted righteous, and he shall bear their iniquities" (Isa. 53:11). That means that you too can be "accounted righteous" by becoming united to Jesus, the Righteous One, by faith.

However it was that Philip explained the gospel, it had its intended effect. This unwelcome outcast found himself being welcomed into the people of God. Indeed he wanted to be marked as belonging to the people of God.

> And as they were going along the road they came to some water, and the eunuch said, "See, here is water! What prevents me from being baptized?" And he commanded the chariot to stop, and they both went down into the water, Philip and the eunuch, and he baptized him. (8:36–38)

Like the Samaritans, he was an outsider, excluded from full participation in the life of Israel. Not only that, he was an outcast, unwelcome in the assembly. And he has been gathered in.

> And when they came up out of the water, the Spirit of the Lord carried Philip away, and the eunuch saw him no more, and went on his way rejoicing. But Philip found himself at Azotus, and as he passed through he preached the gospel to all the towns until he came to Caesarea. (8:39–40)

The eunuch is rejoicing. Perhaps he hardly needed that chariot to carry him back home. Earlier we read that there was "much joy" in the city of Samaria. To be on the outside of all the blessings of belonging to Christ and his people and to be welcomed in—that leads to rejoicing. To be an outcast considered unworthy and unwelcome to approach God for forgiveness and acceptance, and to discover that Christ took your place as one despised and rejected, as one who was crushed for your iniquities so that you can be welcomed in—that leads to rejoicing. Doesn't it just make you want to share this joy with those you know and those with whom you come in contact, who feel that they are on the outside, excluded, unwanted, unworthy?

Courtney was right when she said that I am a gatherer. But one thing this passage shows me is that I have a long way to go to be a gatherer like Jesus is a gatherer. You see, I like to gather my friends, people like me, people who like me, people who like the same things I like, low-maintenance, high fun-factor people. But when I look into this passage, what I see is that Jesus is at work through those who have identified themselves with him to gather people who are nothing like them—people on the margins, outcasts, outsiders, messy people who are going to require some investment of time and energy. Frankly, isn't it just easier for us to be content with gathering in people like us—people in a similar socioeconomic class, people with the same ethnic background, people with similar political and cultural views and assumptions? But that simply isn't the way of Jesus. There is simply no place for elitism, exclusion, prejudice, or preference when it comes to who we will seek out and welcome into our lives as brothers and sisters in Christ.

As representatives of Jesus, there is gathering work for us to do, and for now, there is time to do it. The season for gathering has not yet passed. But one day it will. One day Jesus will return to this earth to "gather his elect from the four winds, from one end of the heavens to the other" (Matt. 24:31). And until that day, we want to be a part of his gathering work, gladly opening the door to outsiders and outcasts, to the inconvenient and unfamiliar, welcoming them into the family.

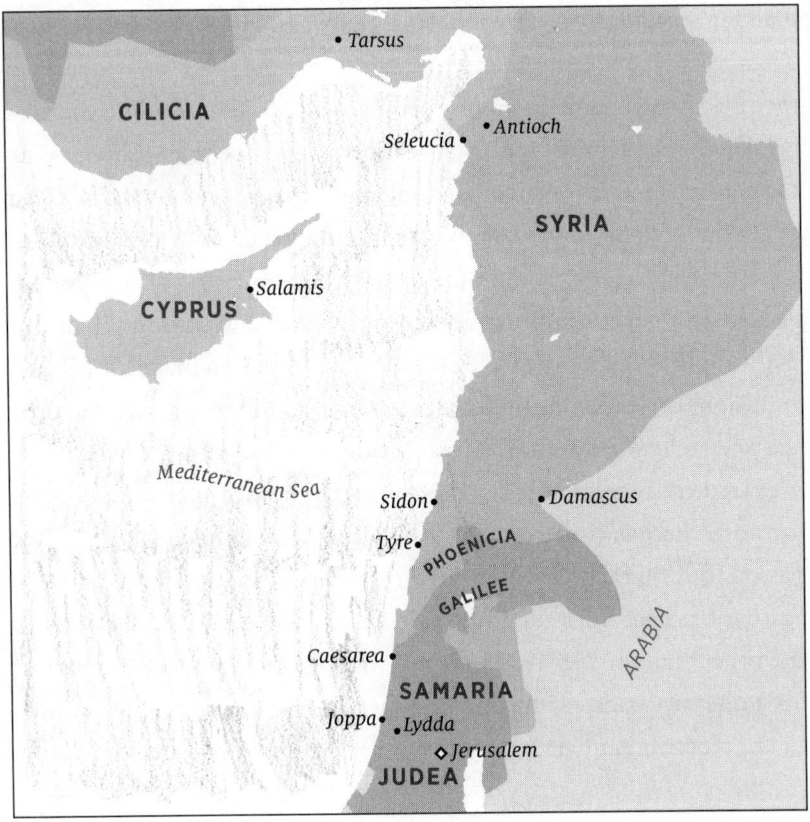

Tarsus
CILICIA
Antioch
Seleucia
SYRIA
Salamis
CYPRUS
Mediterranean Sea
Sidon
Damascus
Tyre
PHOENICIA
GALILEE
ARABIA
Caesarea
SAMARIA
Joppa
Lydda
Jerusalem
JUDEA

7

God's Chosen Instrument

Acts 9:1–31

RECENTLY I LISTENED TO a fascinating interview on Collin Hansen's podcast, *Gospelbound*.[1] It was a ninety-minute conversation with Molly Worthen, a journalist and tenured history professor at the University of North Carolina at Chapel Hill. Over many years, Molly has written as an outsider about evangelical Christians and, when doing so, has sometimes been accused of being "snarky" and having little sympathy for her subjects.[2] Then recently she was asked to write an article on J. D. Greear and the Summit Church.[3] She began talking to people at the church, visiting the church, and sat down to interview J. D. Over time she felt herself increasingly drawn into the church and began an email correspondence with Greear to get her more personal questions about faith answered. She asked him for recommendations of books to read and began reading the books he recommended:

---

1 Collin Hansen, "What Happened to Historian Molly Worthen?" *Gospelbound* podcast, The Gospel Coalition, May 9, 2023, https://www.thegospelcoalition.org/.

2 R. Albert Mohler Jr., "Apostles of Reason: The Crisis of Authority in American Evangelicalism," The Gospel Coalition, November 8, 2013, https://www.thegospelcoalition.org/.

3 Molly Worthen, "The Soul Truth," *The Assembly*, April 28, 2022, https://www.theassemblync.com/.

I found myself more than 51 percent persuaded that the Christian account of the resurrection is the best account we have. But I couldn't believe that a person could be converted by reading a lot of books. . . . I was praying for some sort of warm and fuzzy mystical intervention, and it didn't happen. I just got to the point as a consistent pragmatist that I had to admit I had gotten over that line of the resurrection being the best explanation for the historical evidence, which meant I had to change my working hypothesis of the universe. That weekend I switched from praying, "God show yourself to me," to "Jesus, you are my Lord and Savior."[4]

"Is my conversion real?" she asks. "You don't hear about a lot of people saved through reading a lot of footnotes. . . . But I have this longing to read Scripture—especially the Gospels—that I never had before, and I think, 'that is not me. That is new.' "[5]

Isn't it interesting how God saves people? And whom God saves? And how he changes them? It's often the people we least expect and in a way we would never expect. Some people hear the gospel and immediately take hold of it, while others spend a lot of time considering the claims of Christ and gradually come to faith. Some people have a profoundly emotional experience, while others feel very little. Some experience immediate deliverance from sinful impulses and patterns, while others spend a lifetime seeking to put certain sins to death. But there is one thing that is always the same. No matter who it happens to or how it comes about, salvation is always a supernatural work of God in which blind eyes are opened, giving a person the ability to see who Jesus is and the faith to trust him.

As we work our way through Acts, we're talking about salvation— God's salvation that is being offered to all people. We've seen God's salvation purposes and power in Jerusalem and then move out to Judea

4   Hansen, "*What Happened to Historian Molly Worthen?*"
5   Hansen, "*What Happened to Historian Molly Worthen?*"

and Samaria. And we know where this salvation message is headed from there—to the ends of the earth. But how is that going to happen? In this chapter we meet the person who is going to be the chief conduit of the salvation message that will penetrate the known world that surrounds Judea and Samaria.

If we're familiar with the Bible's story, we're not surprised to discover who that is. But if we were living in the days that are recorded for us in the book of Acts, we would be completely surprised. God's choice is surely the last person any of the Christians in his day would have expected God to save, let alone choose as his representative to the world.

Saved in Spite of Past Resistance

Saul grew up in the busy streets and crowded bazaars of the city of Tarsus, a Greek city devoted to learning.[6] Though Saul's family lived in a Greek city, they were Jewish. In fact, as Saul would write later, he was "a Hebrew of Hebrews" (Phil. 3:5), circumcised on the eighth day. On that day, he was given a double name—Saul, the name of his ancestor, the first king of Israel, for the Jewish part of his life; and Paul, a Greek name for his life of trade in a Greek city.

By the time he was five years old, Saul was probably already learning to read the scrolls of the Old Testament. At six, he would have begun to be schooled by a rabbi to become immersed in the law. We know that between the ages of thirteen and sixteen, Saul was sent to Jerusalem to study under a respected teacher of the law, Gamaliel.

At some point, Saul began to encounter followers of "the Way"—Jews who believed that Jesus of Nazareth was the Messiah and had risen from the dead and ascended into heaven. To Saul and so many of his fellow Pharisees, this was blasphemy worthy of the death penalty. Saul became active in an effort to squash what he saw as a perversion of the Jewish faith. Evidently, the religious leaders in Jerusalem took note

6 This paragraph and others in this chapter are adapted from Nancy Guthrie, *Saints and Scoundrels in the Story of Jesus* (Wheaton, IL: Crossway, 2019), 189–95. Used by permission.

of Saul's zeal and put him in charge of the no-holds-barred offensive against any and all who had turned away from righteousness through law-keeping (as taught by the rabbis) and toward righteousness through faith in the risen Jesus.

We see our first glimpse of Saul as he stands and watches the men of Jerusalem hurl huge stones at Stephen that broke his bones, bloodied his body, and eventually took his life. We read in Acts 8:1 that "Saul approved of his execution." But perhaps that is an understatement. Evidently, it whetted Saul's appetite for more. We read that "Saul was ravaging the church, and entering house after house, he dragged off men and women and committed them to prison" (8:3).

Perhaps you've seen a movie in which Nazi soldiers break into a home, drag away young and old alike, and load them onto a train to be herded into a prison camp or gas chamber. Saul seems to fit right in with the coldest, cruelest characters we've ever seen in movies as we read the opening verses of Acts 9.

But Saul, still breathing threats and murder against the disciples of the Lord, went to the high priest and asked him for letters to the synagogues at Damascus, so that if he found any belonging to the Way, men or women, he might bring them bound to Jerusalem." (9:1–2)

Hatred for Jesus and those who were connected to him was such a part of Saul that he ate and slept and breathed out that hatred. It was not enough for him to put the Christians in Jerusalem and its surrounding cities in prison. He was out to chase down and snuff out Jews who had fled to foreign cities. So he set his sights on the nearest large city outside the borders of Palestine and packed his bags. He put together a group of men who would not hesitate to drag old men out of their beds and mothers away from their children. He was going to tie them up and march them back in chains to Jerusalem, and if any of them should not survive the trip, it was of no concern to him. He was a hunter of human beings, and he was good at it.

He had no moral quandary about it. He was convinced that Jesus was dead and that what he was doing was right. He had the letter in his pocket from the high priest in Jerusalem that he planned to present to the leaders of the synagogue in Damascus. He would compel them to name the names of those who had dared to speak about Jesus in the synagogue or who were gathering on the first day of the week because they claimed Jesus was raised on the first day of the week.

Now as he went on his way, he approached Damascus, and suddenly a light from heaven shone around him. (9:3)

It was the middle of the day. The sun was in the sky, but this was not the sun; it was "a light from heaven, brighter than the sun" (Acts 26:13). This light from heaven was, in fact, the radiant glory of the face of the risen Jesus shining down so brightly on Saul that he was blinded by it. The human features of Jesus were looking down on Saul through the open doorway of heaven.

And falling to the ground, he heard a voice saying to him, "Saul, Saul, why are you persecuting me?" And he said, "Who are you, Lord?" And he said, "I am Jesus, whom you are persecuting." (9:4–5)

Surely Saul would have preferred any other answer to his question than the one he received. The Jesus that he thought was dead was clearly not dead. And not only was he not dead; he was the living Lord of the universe! And he took personally Saul's assault on those who had put their hope in him. There, with his face to the ground, it began to dawn on Saul that Jesus was so united to those who loved and believed in him that every cruel thing Saul had done to any one of them, he had done to Jesus.

The men who were traveling with him stood speechless, hearing the voice but seeing no one. Saul rose from the ground, and although his eyes were opened, he saw nothing. So they led him by the hand and brought him into Damascus. And for three days he was without sight, and neither ate nor drank. (9:7–9)

What must have gone through Saul's mind as he sat in the dark for those three days? F. B. Meyer writes about this time: "It is an awful discovery when a great light from heaven shows a man that what he has regarded his solemn duty has been one long sin against the dearest purposes of God."[7]

Chosen to Carry the Name of Christ

While Saul experienced a supernatural revelation of who Jesus is, someone else in the city of Damascus was also receiving supernatural revelation.

Now there was a disciple at Damascus named Ananias. The Lord said to him in a vision, "Ananias." And he said, "Here I am, Lord." And the Lord said to him, "Rise and go to the street called Straight, and at the house of Judas look for a man of Tarsus named Saul, for behold, he is praying, and he has seen in a vision a man named Ananias come in and lay his hands on him so that he might regain his sight." But Ananias answered, "Lord, I have heard from many about this man, how much evil he has done to your saints at Jerusalem. And here he has authority from the chief priests to bind all who call on your name." (9:10–14)

Word had made it all the way to Damascus—not just about the harm that had been done by Saul to believers in Jerusalem, but about his

7 F. B. Meyer, *Saul: A Servant of Jesus Christ* (Fort Washington, PA: Christian Literature Crusade, 1983), 42.

plan to put the believers in Damascus in chains and drag them back to Jerusalem to be imprisoned or executed. Imagine the fear in the homes of believers in Damascus. Surely they were praying for protection from Saul, praying that he would not lay hands on them to drag them away. And then Ananias was told to go and lay hands on Saul, not to harm him, but to heal him.

> But the Lord said to him, "Go, for he is a chosen instrument of mine to carry my name before the Gentiles and kings and the children of Israel. For I will show him how much he must suffer for the sake of my name." (9:15–16)

chosen instrument of mine

Chosen instrument? This must have been shocking to Ananias. Out of all the people in the world that God could choose to use to make the gospel of Jesus Christ known, Saul was the one God had chosen?

Later Saul will write to the church in Galatia that he was "set apart" before he was born for the very purpose of preaching Christ amongst the Gentiles. Think about that. If Saul was set apart for this purpose before he was born, then we realize that God was sovereign over every day of his life up to this point. God had been working out his plan for Saul—in his timing—over the course of a life mired in sin. (Isn't God's timing in salvation an amazing thing? And don't we sometimes wish he would save people in our timing?) Over his lifetime up to this point, God was preparing him to fulfill the purpose he had for him. Being raised in a Gentile city prepared him to take the gospel to Gentiles. Being schooled in the Scriptures prepared him to make his case to the Jews from the Scriptures. Having been given two names at birth, one for his Jewish life and one for his life in the marketplace, equipped him to become Paul, the apostle to the Gentiles. And being gripped by rage and self-righteousness prepared him to cherish the gospel of grace so that he will one day write, "Formerly I was a blasphemer, persecutor, and insolent opponent. But I received mercy because I had acted ignorantly in unbelief, and the grace of our Lord overflowed for me with the faith and love that are in Christ Jesus" (1 Tim. 1:13–14).

Saved by Supernatural Sight

I think that if I were Ananias, I would have dragged my feet in carrying out this mission of searching out the church's chief persecutor. But not Ananias.

> So Ananias departed and entered the house. And laying his hands on him he said, "Brother Saul, the Lord Jesus who appeared to you on the road by which you came has sent me so that you may regain your sight and be filled with the Holy Spirit." And immediately something like scales fell from his eyes, and he regained his sight. (9:17–18)

This isn't the first time Luke has written about Jesus healing physical blindness as a way of demonstrating his power to heal spiritual blindness. In Luke 4, at the outset of his ministry, we find Jesus picking up the scroll of Isaiah in his hometown and reading, "The Spirit of the Lord is upon me. . . . He has sent me to proclaim liberty to the captives and recovering of sight to the blind" (Luke 4:18). In Luke 7, we read that as Jesus continued his ministry, "on many who were blind he bestowed sight" (v. 21). As he passed through Jericho on his way to Jerusalem where he would be crucified, Jesus healed the blind man beside the road who cried out to him (Luke 18:35–43). And after his resurrection, as he ate with the two followers he had walked with on the road to Emmaus, "their eyes were opened, and they recognized him" (Luke 24:31). Here again, we see that Jesus is still at work from his throne in heaven. Jesus has opened the blind eyes of Saul. As the scales fell from his eyes, Saul could see that for all his life he had been living in spiritual darkness. Everything he had lived for had been all wrong. He was no longer filled with murderous rage. Instead, he was filled with the Holy Spirit.

Then he rose and was baptized; and taking food, he was strengthened. For some days he was with the disciples at Damascus. (9:18–19)

The blasphemer has become a baptized believer. The one who had been breathing threats against them has become the brother beside them.

And immediately he proclaimed Jesus in the synagogues, saying, "He is the Son of God." (9:20)

The religious predator has become gospel preacher!

And all who heard him were amazed and said, "Is not this the man who made havoc in Jerusalem of those who called upon this name? And has he not come here for this purpose, to bring them bound before the chief priests?" But Saul increased all the more in strength, and confounded the Jews who lived in Damascus by proving that Jesus was the Christ. (9:21–22)

Imagine being in this circle of believers in Damascus. The person who had been breathing threats and murder was now proclaiming life in Jesus. Rather than leaning on the Old Testament to justify his murder of Christians, he was showing everyone who would listen that Jesus is the fulfillment of everything the Old Testament promised that the Christ would be and do.

Saved to Face Hostility and Opposition

The believers in Damascus must have been skeptical initially but then slowly came around to celebrate the supernatural change that had taken place in Saul. The unbelieving Jews in Damascus, however, were not at all happy with this change. They became determined to do to Saul what Saul had originally planned to do to the believers in Damascus.

When many days had passed, the Jews plotted to kill him, but their plot became known to Saul. They were watching the gates day and night in order to kill him, but his disciples took him by night and let him down through an opening in the wall, lowering him in a basket. (9:23–25)

Saul slipped away from Damascus and eventually made his way back to Jerusalem,[8] where he faced some of the same skepticism from believers that he had experienced in Damascus.

And when he had come to Jerusalem, he attempted to join the disciples. And they were all afraid of him, for they did not believe that he was a disciple. (9:26)

I get that. Don't you? Surely the memory of him watching everyone's coats as a mob hurled stones at Stephen was still very fresh.

But Barnabas took him and brought him to the apostles and declared to them how on the road he had seen the Lord, who spoke to him, and how at Damascus he had preached boldly in the name of Jesus. So he went in and out among them at Jerusalem, preaching boldly in the name of the Lord. (9:27–28)

Fear among the disciples gave way to fellowship. Keeping Saul at arm's length gave way to linking arms with him to face whatever opposition might come for boldly preaching that Jesus is the Christ.

But once again, not everyone in town was so accepting of this change in Saul. Imagine how angry the religious council must have been when they heard that Saul, their champion Christian-hunter, had joined forces with the Christians! No longer was he breathing threats and

---

8 See Gal. 1:15–24 for Paul's account of this time.

murder against them; he was proclaiming Christ with them. He no longer hated them and their Christ; he loved them and their Christ. He was no longer in league with the Jews in Jerusalem. Instead, he was exposing all the faults in their arguments against Jesus as the Christ. And it made them murderously mad.

> And he spoke and disputed against the Hellenists. But they were seeking to kill him. And when the brothers learned this, they brought him down to Caesarea and sent him off to Tarsus. (9:29–30)

Saul has gone from hunter to hunted. The Christians in Jerusalem have gone from being persecuted by Saul to protecting Saul from persecution. Saul is sent off to his hometown of Tarsus, not with intentions to capture Christ followers and bring them back to Jerusalem in chains, but to proclaim Christ where he is not known and invite people to become a part of Christ's kingdom.

As we take in this amazing story, we realize that God saves all kinds of people in all kinds of ways. He saved Saul by blinding him with the light of the face of the glorified Jesus so that Saul would believe that he really did rise from the dead. Molly Worthen would say that she was saved as she slowly became convinced that Jesus rose from the dead. I would say that I was saved as the Spirit worked through the preached word at my church so that when I was eight years old, I understood my need for Christ and took hold of him by faith. How about you? How did God save you?

The truth is, anyone who is saved is saved the same way. It is always supernatural, though it might appear to be quite ordinary. It doesn't have to be sensational to be supernatural. It doesn't have to be emotional to be supernatural. Some people can tell you the moment when everything changed, and they became convinced and clear on who Jesus is. Others can't tell you exactly when it happened. But that doesn't mean it didn't. Whether or not a person knows exactly *when* it happened, there is always a moment in the secret place of the soul when a person who is saved went from being spiritually dead to spiritually alive, separated from Christ to joined to Christ (Eph. 2:1–7).

Indeed, if you have experienced the salvation made available through faith in Christ, I can tell you that your salvation was like Saul's salvation in a number of ways.

- Like Saul, God saved you in spite of past defiance, past apathy, past unbelief, past rejection of Christ, past sin against Christ.

- Like Saul, you were saved through a supernatural experience of having your eyes opened to who Jesus is and why you must become united to him by faith. Maybe your eyes were opened suddenly like Saul, or maybe it was more slowly, like Molly. However it happened, and however long it took, it was equally as supernatural.

- Like Saul, your salvation may lead to persecution. You may face opposition from your family, your coworkers, and your community. That opposition may hurt you, it may discourage you, it may frighten you. But don't let it silence you. You will never regret anything you might lose because of your public devotion to Jesus Christ. He will see to that.

- Like Saul, you have been saved for the purpose of enjoying Jesus and proclaiming that joy found in him wherever he places you, whether that is in a toddler play group, a neighborhood association, a teachers' lounge, a business office, a family gathering, an exercise class, a bridge club, a retirement home, or a nursing home.

God chose you and saved you to carry his name into places and to people whose eyes have not yet been opened. Perhaps the Spirit will use your words to heal the blindness of people you know so that they can see the beauty, sufficiency, and necessity of Jesus. Wouldn't that be thrilling?

Sea of
Galilee

• Caesarea

• Sebaste (Samaria)

SAMARIA

Mediterranean Sea

• Antipatris

• Joppa

Jordan
River

• Lydda

◇ Jerusalem

JUDEA

Dead
Sea

TO ETHIOPIA

8

What God Has Made Clean

Acts 9:32–11:18

THE FIRST SEMINARY CLASS I TOOK at Reformed Theological Seminary was church history. I read the guide to preparation for the midterm, and it said, "Know the significant dates." I made a chart of the key dates covered in the first half of the course and what happened on those significant dates. But as I prepared for the midterm, I assumed that when it said, "Know the dates," it meant, you know, "Be very familiar with the dates. Have a general sense of when things happened." It wasn't until I logged on to take the midterm and I was asked to give the specific dates for a series of events in early church history that I realized that when the study guide said, "Know the dates," it actually meant, "Know. The. Dates." It had been stated clearly, but I just didn't hear it. Perhaps because I didn't want to hear it.

In a similar way, God's intention that his salvation is for people of all nations had been stated clearly throughout the Old Testament. We first get a glimpse of it when we hear him tell Abram, "In you all the families of the earth shall be blessed" (Gen. 12:3). Generations later we see a mixed multitude leave Egypt with the Israelites, marry into the family, and receive a portion of the promised land with everyone else. We witness God going out of his way to draw non-Jews into his family—people like Tamar and Rahab and Ruth.

The psalmists put words on the lips of God's people extolling God's intention to draw people of all nations to worship him. They sang:

> May God be gracious to us and bless us
> and make his face to shine upon us,
> that your way may be known on earth,
> your saving power among all nations.
> Let the peoples praise you, O God;
> let all the peoples praise you! (Ps. 67:1–3)

And the prophets spoke often about a day in the future when the peoples of many nations would come to worship Israel's God. For example, Isaiah wrote:

> It shall come to pass in the latter days
> that the mountain of the house of the LORD
> shall be established as the highest of the mountains,
> and shall be lifted up above the hills;
> and all the nations shall flow to it,
> and many peoples shall come, and say:
> "Come, let us go up to the mountain of the LORD,
> to the house of the God of Jacob." (Isa. 2:2–3)

The very purpose of Israel being set apart from other nations was so that other nations would see how good it was to have Yahweh as their God and would come to Yahweh for salvation. But somewhere along the way, the privilege of being set apart by God to be his instrument in the world to draw all peoples turned into prejudice against all peoples. Privilege morphed into pride, the kind of pride that caused Jewish people to look down on, even despise, Gentiles. The food laws that made it difficult to share a meal with Gentiles became an excuse to detest and avoid Gentiles. This is the world of Jewish presumption and ethnic pride that Jesus entered into when he was born as a Jew. Jesus, however, made it clear that while he came first to the Jews, he intended that his salvation would be declared to people of every nation, instructing his disciples as he ascended into heaven, "Go therefore and make disciples of *all nations*" (Matt. 28:19).

So the plan and command and expectation had been clear throughout the Old Testament, and it had been clear from Jesus's own lips. The apostles heard it. But they didn't get it. Or maybe, like me, when I heard "know the dates" and really didn't want to memorize them, they just really didn't want to take the gospel to Gentile people and nations. In their minds, Gentiles needed to become Jews before they could come anywhere close to getting in on God's salvation through Christ. That meant the men had to be circumcised, and they had to take up following the Jewish calendar and rituals. This was a huge assumption—a mistaken assumption—on their part. The apostles didn't get that salvation is for *all* who will repent and believe in Christ, with no hoops added for non-Jews to jump through. At least they didn't get it so far in the story Acts has told us. But that is about to change.

Peter Is Authenticated as Carrying on the Ministry of Jesus

Throughout Acts we've been reading that the apostles have been doing healing miracles that authenticated their message of salvation through Jesus. As we come to the final two paragraphs of Acts 9, we read about two miracles performed by Peter as he makes his way from Jerusalem to the coast of the Mediterranean Sea.

While Peter was at the center of the story Acts tells us in chapters 1–5, it is Stephen, Philip, and Saul who have dominated the narrative since then. So why are we back to Peter? If there is going to be as big of a shift as there needs to be in terms of understanding how God is working out his salvation plans in the world, Peter, the leader of the apostles, is going to have to be a part of it.

Aeneas

> Now as Peter went here and there among them all, he came down also to the saints who lived at Lydda. There he found a man named Aeneas, bedridden for eight years, who was paralyzed. And Peter said to him, "Aeneas, Jesus Christ heals you; rise and make your bed." And immediately he rose. And all the residents of Lydda and Sharon saw him, and they turned to the Lord. (9:32–35)

Here is a man who everyone knows has been paralyzed for a long time. Peter announces that Jesus has healed him and tells him to rise and pick up his bed. And he does. It reminds us of a miracle during the ministry of Jesus, doesn't it, when Jesus healed the paralytic and told him to pick up his bed and walk?

Tabitha

Then in verses 36–43, we read about a woman named Tabitha who has died. Everyone is standing around weeping. Peter puts them all outside and then says to the deceased woman, "Tabitha, arise" (9:40). He takes her by the hand, and she is raised to life again. You could not hear this story and miss that it is just like when Jesus raised up Jairus's daughter. In fact, Peter's words are only one Greek letter different from those of Jesus. Whereas Jesus said, "Talitha, arise" (Mark 5:41), Peter says, "Tabitha, arise."

The similarity of these two miracles to miracles of Jesus serves to authenticate the ministry of Peter, making clear that Jesus is at work *through* his apostle. But the next scene shows us that Jesus is also at work *in* his apostle.

Peter Is Corrected on Who Can Get in on the Salvation of Jesus

There is something Peter needs to see, something he needs to understand that he may have heard before, but it just hasn't become clear to him yet. It is so significant that it's going to require supernatural revelation for Peter to receive it. Peter, however, is not the first one in this story who receives supernatural revelation.

Peter ∞

> At Caesarea there was a man named Cornelius, a centurion of what was known as the Italian Cohort, a devout man who feared God with all his household, gave alms generously to the people, and prayed continually to God. (10:1–2)

Cornelius

uncircumsize

Caesarea is about 33 miles up the coast from where Peter is staying in Joppa. In this town resides a commander of a cohort of one hundred Roman soldiers. Luke tells us he "fears God," which designates Cornelius as belonging to a special category of non-Jews who believed in Israel's God and went to the synagogue but had not become full converts to Judaism, which required submission to the rite of circumcision and adherence to the dietary restrictions in the Levitical commands. He is, however, devout. He is noted for his charitable gifts to the poor and his constant prayer. But he's still uncircumcised, and because of that, Jews would've considered him unclean and therefore would not have socialized with him. He may be honorable, but he's still, in their view, unclean.

> About the ninth hour of the day he saw clearly in a vision an angel of God come in and say to him, "Cornelius." And he stared at him in terror and said, "What is it, Lord?" And he said to him, "Your prayers and your alms have ascended as a memorial before God. And now send men to Joppa and bring one Simon who is called Peter. He is lodging with one Simon, a tanner, whose house is by the sea." When the angel who spoke to him had departed, he called two of his servants and a devout soldier from among those who attended him, and having related everything to them, he sent them to Joppa. (10:3–8)

Went for Peter

Imagine what it must have meant to this God-fearing Gentile for an angel to appear to him, telling him that God has heard and been pleased by his prayers. Evidently, however, there is something missing in Cornelius's devout life—something so significant that the veil between heaven and earth has been pierced so that it can be dealt with. Cornelius is sincere. But Cornelius is not saved.

Meanwhile Peter also receives divine revelation because there is something missing in his apostolic ministry—something so significant that the veil between heaven and earth is pierced so that it can be dealt with.

> The next day, as they were on their journey and approaching the city, Peter went up on the housetop about the sixth hour to pray. And he became hungry and wanted something to eat, but while they were preparing it, he fell into a trance and saw the heavens opened and something like a great sheet descending, being let down by its four corners upon the earth. In it were all kinds of animals and reptiles and birds of the air. And there came a voice to him: "Rise, Peter; kill and eat." But Peter said, "By no means, Lord; for I have never eaten anything that is common or unclean." And the voice came to him again a second time, "What God has made clean, do not call common." This happened three times, and the thing was taken up at once to heaven. (10:9–16)

Peter has gone to the housetop to pray, and he's hungry. But Peter has never, throughout the whole of his life, been able to simply eat whatever he wants when hunger strikes. There are whole categories of foods that have been off limits based on the Levitical food laws found in Leviticus 11. No camel jerky. No rock badger burgers. No bacon, lettuce, and tomato sandwiches. No shrimp cocktail.

It had not yet become clear to Peter and the rest of the new-covenant community that the life, death, and resurrection of Jesus had made Levitical food laws obsolete. They had always been provisional, established as pointers toward the day when true cleansing would be made available for all peoples through the blood of Jesus. Jesus had said, "There is nothing outside a person that by going into him can defile him, but the things that come out of a person are what defile him" (Mark 7:15). The apostles heard this. But they were still holding to what had been a way of life for them.

We can almost hear Peter's pride in his lifelong strict observance of these laws when he says, "*By no means, Lord*; for I have never eaten anything that is common or unclean" (10:14).

The voice of God from heaven tells Peter, "What God has made clean, do not call common." In fact, because this is evidently so challenging for Peter to process, God says the same thing three times.

Verse 17 tells us that Peter was "inwardly perplexed" about what the vision meant. We can almost see him on the housetop with his brow furrowed, evidencing intense thought.

> And while Peter was pondering the vision, the Spirit said to him, "Behold, three men are looking for you. Rise and go down and accompany them without hesitation, for I have sent them." (10:19–20)

The men at the gate told Peter about how the angel appeared to Cornelius and how the angel told him to send for Peter so Cornelius could "hear what you have to say" (10:22). Peter has been summoned by the Spirit to go to this God-fearing Gentile house to give him a message.

Had Peter not had the vision, he certainly would never have accepted this invitation. He just didn't go to Gentile homes and accept their hospitality. Who knew what was in those sandwiches? But the Spirit had spoken, so the next day he and some other believers living in Joppa went to Caesarea.

When Peter arrived at the home of Cornelius, he discovered that a number of relatives and close friends had joined him, anxious to hear what the man summoned by the angel would have to say.

And he said to them, "You yourselves know how unlawful it is for a Jew to associate with or to visit anyone of another nation." (10:28a)

When Peter says it is "unlawful" for a Jew to associate with anyone of another nation, he's not saying that the Old Testament Levitical law forbade this. It didn't. But that is how it was interpreted in his day. Because Gentiles didn't follow the same food laws, it had become socially and religiously unacceptable for Jews to associate with people of other nations.

"But God has shown me that I should not call any person common or unclean. So when I was sent for, I came without objection. I ask then why you sent for me." (10:28b–29)

We might expect that Peter would say, "God has shown me that I should not call any *foods* common or unclean." But the vision, combined with the Spirit-instructed visit to the home of a Gentile, has enabled Peter to understand the purpose or point of the vision. He understands that God is revealing to him that Gentiles are no longer to be considered unclean.

With this fresh understanding, the gospel is reaching even further into Peter's life than it had to this point. It is invading the place where ethnic and national pride sits, prejudice that is so much a part of the fabric of a person that it seems impossible to separate it from the person. But it's got to go so the gospel can spread. It's got to go because ethnic superiority, favoritism, and prejudice simply have no place among people who carry the name of Jesus. Here is Peter, the rock on whom Jesus intends to build his church, a church made up of people from every nation. This attachment to Gentile derision and exclusion is a hurdle that simply must be overcome.

So Peter opened his mouth and said: "Truly I understand that God shows no partiality, but in every nation anyone who fears him and does what is right is acceptable to him. As for the word that he sent to Israel, preaching good news of peace through Jesus Christ (he is Lord of all), you yourselves know what happened throughout all Judea, beginning from Galilee after the baptism that John proclaimed: how God anointed Jesus of Nazareth with the Holy Spirit and with power. He went about doing good and healing all who were oppressed by the devil, for God was with him. And we are witnesses of all that he did both in the country of the Jews and in Jerusalem. They put him to death by hanging him on a tree, but God raised him on the third day and made him to appear, not to all the people but to us who had been chosen by God as witnesses, who ate and drank with him after he rose from the dead. And he commanded us to preach to the people and to testify that he is the one appointed by God to be judge of the living and the dead. To him all the prophets bear witness that everyone who believes in him receives forgiveness of sins through his name." (10:34–43)

Essentially Peter delivers the same gospel message to the Gentiles that he gave to the Jews gathered in Jerusalem at Pentecost. He tells them about Jesus's righteous life, his atoning death, his victorious resurrection, his present reign and future return as judge of the living and the dead. This announcement of who Jesus is and what he has done is followed by how these Gentiles can get in on the benefits of being joined to Jesus by faith. Anyone and everyone who puts their faith in Jesus receives forgiveness of sins. As cleansed and forgiven sinners, they can approach God, not as outsiders, not as second-class citizens, but with confidence that they will be welcomed.

While Peter was still saying these things, the Holy Spirit fell on all who heard the word. And the believers from among the circumcised who had come with Peter were amazed, because the gift of the Holy Spirit was poured out even on the Gentiles. For they were hearing them speaking in tongues and extolling God. Then Peter declared, "Can anyone withhold water for baptizing these people, who have received the Holy Spirit just as we have?" And he commanded them to be baptized in the name of Jesus Christ. Then they asked him to remain for some days. (10:44–48)

These new Gentile believers experienced the same baptism of the Holy Spirit and water baptism that the Jewish believers experienced at Pentecost. They're now full-fledged members of the new-covenant community of those who are joined to Christ by faith.

Imagine what it was like for Peter and the Jews who came with him to Caesarea as they spent several days staying in the homes of these Gentile believers. That was new. Eating with them—that was new. Growing to love them—that was new too. They had never called Gentiles "brothers" before.

And imagine how those days were for Cornelius and his friends and family. They had always been on the fringes, and now they've been welcomed in. They had only known the duty of seeking to be devout God fearers. Now they're experiencing the joy of being forgiven, indwelt by the Holy Spirit, growing in love for their Savior, Jesus Christ. Now they're experiencing grace.

Peter Is Heard by Those Who Have Limited the Salvation of Jesus

Peter and the Jews who were with him who witnessed the descent of the Spirit on these Gentiles had no doubt about God's glad welcome of uncircumcised Gentiles into the family. But the Jewish believers back in Jerusalem didn't witness it. And when Peter gets back to Jerusalem, they've got questions.

Now the apostles and the brothers who were throughout Judea heard that the Gentiles also had received the word of God. So when Peter went up to Jerusalem, the circumcision party criticized him, saying,

"You went to uncircumcised men and ate with them." But Peter began and explained it to them in order. (11:1–4)

Peter goes on to recount his vision and command from heaven, telling him three times, "What God has made clean, do not call common" (11:9). He tells them about how the angel appeared to Cornelius, telling him, "Send to Joppa and bring Simon who is called Peter; he will declare to you a message by which you will be saved, you and all your household" (11:13–14). He tells them:

> "As I began to speak, the Holy Spirit fell on them just as on us at the beginning. And I remembered the word of the Lord, how he said, 'John baptized with water, but you will be baptized with the Holy Spirit.' If then God gave the same gift to them as he gave to us when we believed in the Lord Jesus Christ, who was I that I could stand in God's way?" (11:15–17)

I wonder if, at that point, Peter held his breath to hear how his Jewish brothers and sisters would respond. Perhaps he continued to wonder as they all sat in silence for a while, evidently thinking it through. And then something beautiful happened. Something that would quite literally change the world.

> And they glorified God, saying, "Then to the Gentiles also God has granted repentance that leads to life." (11:18)

When we read those words, what we must recognize is that what we're reading not only impacted the Gentiles in the first century; it impacts you and me today. The reason those of us who are not Jews have heard the gospel and have been welcomed to respond to that good news in repentance and faith, and have had the Holy Spirit come to dwell in us, is that the original witnesses—the twelve apostles—listened to what

Peter had to say about his experience with the Gentiles being granted repentance and receiving the Spirit. God has granted repentance that leads to life—even to people like you and me!

Indeed, this repentance that leads to life isn't simply something we look back on as a one-time experience, when we went from death to life spiritually. This repentance that leads to life is an ongoing thing as the Spirit works in us revealing our sin to us. Perhaps it is a good thing that God does not show us all our sin or cause us to feel the full weight of it when we first turn to him in repentance. We couldn't bear it. But he is good to show it to us as we continue in the word so we can continue to come under conviction and repent.

And I wonder if the Spirit might be using this word in Acts 10 and 11 to show you something you need to see about yourself. Has God used this word to show you something in yourself that simply has to go—something like ethnic superiority or favoritism or prejudice? You and I will probably not experience an angel showing us the ugliness of attitudes like this that are so much a part of us that we don't even recognize they're there. But we do have his word before us, and the Spirit in us, and so we pray, "Lord, I am the one who is unclean. Please show me the reality of my own heart in regard to people I look down on and avoid. Cleanse away all of the ugliness of my attitudes and actions toward those who don't look like me and think like me and live like me. Save me from pride and exclusivity. May the generosity of your grace toward me make me generous in sharing that grace with everyone you put in front of me."

Tarsus
CILICIA
Antioch
Seleucia
SYRIA
Salamis
CYPRUS
Mediterranean Sea
Sidon
Damascus
Tyre
PHOENICIA
GALILEE
ARABIA
Caesarea
SAMARIA
Joppa
Lydda
Jerusalem
JUDEA

9

The Hand of the Lord Was with Them

Acts 11:19–12:25

IN 1942 DAVIS ELLIS was hired as educational director for the Allstate Insurance Company. His job was to recruit and train female insurance agents during World War II. In 1950 Ellis's daughter got sick with hepatitis. One morning as Dave headed out the door to work, the family physician called to let the family know that he was very concerned about JoAnn and that he was calling in a specialist, a Dr. Keyser. That evening when Ellis returned home, his wife, Helen, rushed to him and threw her arms around him. "Dave," she said, "the specialist has examined [JoAnn] and Dr. Cummings tells me that JoAnn is in good hands with Dr. Keyser."

JoAnn recovered, and later that year, Ellis was part of a group working into the night to plan Allstate's ad program for the coming year. Dave Ellis remembered how his anxiety eased when hearing those words: *in good hands*. He suggested using it as a slogan, along with an illustration of a pair of hands cradling a car. "You're in good hands" has been Allstate's slogan ever since.[1]

---

1   This story of how Allstate's slogan was developed is adapted from "The Good Hands: How a Pivotal Family Moment Inspired Allstate's Longstanding Symbol of Protection," accessed October 4, 2023, https://www.allstatecorporation.com/.

I think Dave Ellis is right that there is something comforting about knowing that you're in good hands, don't you? But, honestly, I think I want more than to simply put my life in the hands of an insurance company, don't you? I want it to be in stronger hands, more secure hands. As we face life in an uncertain world, we need to know that we are in the hands of the one who controls all things, the one who has the power to bring about his purposes in the world and in our lives. We want to be in the hands of the Lord who saves. These are the hands we see at work in Acts 11 and 12.

The Hand of the Lord with His People

Back in chapter 8, we read that the persecution that arose after the stoning of Stephen caused believers in Jerusalem to be "scattered throughout the regions of Judea and Samaria" (8:1). Now we see that that same persecution sent some of them even farther.

> Now those who were scattered because of the persecution that arose over Stephen traveled as far as Phoenicia and Cyprus and Antioch, speaking the word to no one except Jews. But there were some of them, men of Cyprus and Cyrene, who on coming to Antioch spoke to the Hellenists also, preaching the Lord Jesus. (11:19–20)

If you look at a map, you'll see that most who scattered from Jerusalem went to regions just beyond the boundaries of Judea and Samaria where now they are sharing the good news of Jesus with their fellow Jews who live in these regions. But Luke wants us to focus in on some who were originally from the island of Cyprus and the North African country of Cyrene and have gone all the way to Antioch in Syria. This was a large Syrian city that "had a reputation in Rome as an exporter of moral vice."[2] Here they are speaking not only to Jews. They're talking

---

2   Guy Prentiss Waters, *A Study Commentary on the Acts of the Apostles* (Leyland, UK: Evangelical Press, 2015), 278.

about Jesus to Gentiles in the city,[3] which means that they are crossing a greater boundary than simply the boundary between countries.
They're crossing the boundary between Jew and Gentile, which has
always been a huge chasm. And these are not God-fearing Gentiles,
like the Ethiopian eunuch and Cornelius. These are pagan Gentiles
who likely worshiped a vast array of gods.

But they are not on their own. They're in good hands.

And the hand of the Lord was with them, and a great number who
believed turned to the Lord. (11:21)

This is amazing! They spoke and God saved. These ordinary believers
spoke about the one true God becoming flesh and blood and living a
righteous life, dying an atoning death, and rising from the dead. They
told the pagan Gentiles that they could get in on the new life that is
found only in Christ if they would forsake their pagan gods and embrace Christ. And the response was incredible. A "great number" said,
Yes! We want in on that.

How do we explain that? The passage tells us. The hand of the Lord
worked through the presentation of his word. Indeed, this is always
how people are saved. This should actually be very instructive and
encouraging to us. The hand of the Lord is with those who present it
and those who hear it. As people hear the word, the hand of the Lord
plucks those who belong to him out of living a life apart from him and
brings them into a new life lived in him and with his people. This means
that even though we're afraid that our presentation may be clumsy or
cheesy or inadequate, we can keep on sharing the gospel. Evidently it
isn't about us and our skill or smoothness or lack of these things. God
is completely sovereign over salvation. We present Jesus, never taking

3   Brian J. Vickers writes, "The conclusion that these Hellenists in chapter 11 are Gentiles is based on
    the reaction of the Jerusalem church—why send Barnabas to check on the conversion of Greek-
    speaking Jews?" *John–Acts*, ESV Expository Commentary (Wheaton, IL: Crossway, 2019), 443.

responsibility for the results—good or bad—knowing that the power
to save is not in our hands; it's in his hands.

> The report of this came to the ears of the church in Jerusalem, and
> they sent Barnabas to Antioch. When he came and saw the grace
> of God, he was glad, and he exhorted them all to remain faithful to
> the Lord with steadfast purpose, for he was a good man, full of the
> Holy Spirit and of faith. And a great many people were added to
> the Lord. (11:22–24)

When the Jerusalem church heard about the conversion of pagan
Gentiles in Antioch, they sent someone to confirm that it was real.
And what evidence does Barnabas discover? He sees the unmistakable
grace of God at work in the lives of these former pagans. They're not
sacrificing to false gods anymore. They're depending on the once for all
sacrifice of Jesus Christ. Grace has come to them in salvation, and it is
at work in them in sanctification. His word to them is to keep moving
forward in the grace that has saved them. "Remain faithful to the Lord
with a steadfast purpose," he exhorts them. What is that purpose? I like
the way Paul puts it in Philippians 3:9: to "be found in him." That's the
goal of the Christian. Having this kind of purpose must have stood out
among the inhabitants of Antioch, marking them as different.

> And in Antioch the disciples were first called Christians. (11:26)

As these new believers sat under the teaching of godly Barnabas and Saul,
who joined him, their lives were changing. The hand of God that had
saved them was at work shaping them into the image of Christ so that
it made sense that they would be called Christ people, or "Christians."
Perhaps they were first called "Christians" by those who wanted to mock
them, and it stuck, becoming an apt description of who and what they
wanted to be—people marked and known for their connection to Christ.

One way we see the grace of God at work *in* them is the way it worked *through* them, generating a radical act of generosity.

> Now in these days prophets came down from Jerusalem to Antioch. And one of them named Agabus stood up and foretold by the Spirit that there would be a great famine over all the world (this took place in the days of Claudius). So the disciples determined, every one according to his ability, to send relief to the brothers living in Judea. And they did so, sending it to the elders by the hand of Barnabas and Saul. (11:27–30)

This was, perhaps, the first time in recorded history that a people group in one part of the world collected money to send, without strings attached, to help another people group in another part of the world.[4] Why would they do this? The hand of the Lord is with them, prompting them, and the grace of God is at work in them. They want to help brothers and sisters in Christ whom they've never met.

The Hand of Herod against God's People

In chapter 12, the scene shifts back to the city of Jerusalem, where we see another sovereign's hands at work.

> About that time Herod the king laid violent hands on some who belonged to the church. (12:1)

This Herod is the nephew of the Herod who killed Jesus. And evidently the same dynamics are at work here as were in play in the killing of Jesus. Similar to when Jesus was put to death, it was the time of an

---

4 James Montgomery Boice writes, "As far as I know, this is the first charitable act of this nature in all recorded history—one race of people collecting money to help another people. No wonder they were first called Christians at Antioch." *Acts: An Expositional Commentary* (Grand Rapids, MI: Baker, 1997), 203.

important Jewish religious festival, which made it just the right time for Herod to do something to endear himself to the Jews, while also making appearances of respecting their sacred feast. Herod decides to put to death some of the leaders of this group that the religious establishment hates in order to curry favor with the Jews.

> He killed James the brother of John with the sword. (12:2)

James was one of Jesus's closest followers, and he had a prophecy hanging over his head. When James and his brother had asked Jesus if they could sit on his right and left hands when he established his kingdom, Jesus told them, "The cup that I drink you will drink, and with the baptism with which I am baptized, you will be baptized" (Mark 10:39). Certainly, when Jesus said it, they could not have understood exactly what he meant, but after the crucifixion, when Jesus drank the cup of the wrath of God and was "baptized" in death, they must have gotten a better sense of it. So Herod killed James, and then:

> When he saw that it pleased the Jews, he proceeded to arrest Peter also. This was during the days of Unleavened Bread. And when he had seized him, he put him in prison, delivering him over to four squads of soldiers to guard him, intending after the Passover to bring him out to the people. So Peter was kept in prison, but earnest prayer for him was made to God by the church. (12:3–5)

Herod's act of murder masquerading as religious observance was evidently a hit with the people. So he intended to do it again with Peter, arresting him, but delaying his execution until after Passover.

The hand of King Herod seems pretty powerful at this point. He has swung his sword and killed James. He has seized Peter and put him in prison, quadrupling the guards since he knows that Peter has slipped out of prison before. So this time Peter is not merely chained to the floor; Herod has him chained to two soldiers, with more at the door. But clearly Herod is not the king with all the power.

> Now when Herod was about to bring him out, on that very night, Peter was sleeping between two soldiers, bound with two chains, and sentries before the door were guarding the prison. And behold, an angel of the Lord stood next to him, and a light shone in the cell. He struck Peter on the side and woke him, saying, "Get up quickly." And the chains fell off his hands. And the angel said to him, "Dress yourself and put on your sandals." And he did so. And he said to him, "Wrap your cloak around you and follow me." And he went out and followed him. He did not know that what was being done by the angel was real, but thought he was seeing a vision. When they had passed the first and the second guard, they came to the iron gate leading into the city. It opened for them of its own accord, and they went out and went along one street, and immediately the angel left him. When Peter came to himself, he said, "Now I am sure that the Lord has sent his angel and rescued me from the hand of Herod and from all that the Jewish people were expecting." (12:6–11)

Peter recognizes that he has been rescued from the hand of Herod by the hand of the Lord Jesus. Notice that Peter contributes nothing to his escape. He is chained and sound asleep. He has to be told to get dressed and to leave the prison cell. He's in a fog as he is led out past two guards and out of the gates that just seem to open up on their own. Peter has not accomplished his own rescue. The hand of the Lord has rescued him from the hand of Herod.

> When he realized this, he went to the house of Mary, the mother of John whose other name was Mark, where many were gathered together and were praying. And when he knocked at the door of the gateway, a servant girl named Rhoda came to answer. Recognizing

Peter's voice, in her joy she did not open the gate but ran in and reported that Peter was standing at the gate. They said to her, "You are out of your mind." But she kept insisting that it was so, and they kept saying, "It is his angel!" But Peter continued knocking, and when they opened, they saw him and were amazed. But motioning to them with his hand to be silent, he described to them how the Lord had brought him out of the prison. And he said, "Tell these things to James and to the brothers." Then he departed and went to another place. (12:12–17)

I think we're meant to see some humor in this. They're in there fervently praying for Peter to be released. And when the answer to their prayers literally knocks on the door, instead of believing it, they leave Peter at the door while they try on other theories for who might be at the door. When they finally let Peter in the locked gate, he's evidently making hand gestures to get them to be quiet so that they won't attract the attention of the four squads of soldiers who are certainly out looking for him.

Now when day came, there was no little disturbance among the soldiers over what had become of Peter. And after Herod searched for him and did not find him, he examined the sentries and ordered that they should be put to death. Then he went down from Judea to Caesarea and spent time there. (12:18–19)

Herod is giving orders, but clearly he is not the king with all of the power. Indeed, the hand of the King of heaven and earth is about to be turned against him.

The Hand of the Lord against Herod

As we've seen the hand of the Lord at work throughout this passage so far, perhaps we should admit that there's a particular way we'd like to see the hand of God at work at this point. We want God to put his fist down and thereby put an end to the opposition that brings suffering to his people. And the truth is, one day he will. In fact, in this final scene, we get a preview of what will one day happen to all who oppose King Jesus and his people.

> Now Herod was angry with the people of Tyre and Sidon, and they came to him with one accord, and having persuaded Blastus, the king's chamberlain, they asked for peace, because their country depended on the king's country for food. (12:20)

Luke doesn't tell us exactly why Herod was angry with the people of the cities of Tyre and Sidon that were north of him. But we know that these cities were dependent on Herod for food, so they're willing to say whatever they need to say to be able to get Herod to open the pantry doors.

> On an appointed day Herod put on his royal robes, took his seat upon the throne, and delivered an oration to them. And the people were shouting, "The voice of a god, and not of a man!" (12:21–22)

The historian Josephus records what happened on this day with more detail,[5] explaining that Herod's royal robe was made of silver so that when he took his seat on his throne in an open-air theater, he mirrored the rays of the sun. He was shining like a god, so they shouted out to

---

5 "He put on a garment made wholly of silver, and of a contexture truly wonderful, and came into the theatre early in the morning; at which time the silver of his garment, being illuminated by the fresh reflection of the sun's rays upon it, shone out after a surprising manner, and was so resplendent as to spread a horror over those that looked intently upon him; and presently his flatterers cried out, one from one place, and another from another (though not for his good), that he was a god. . . . A severe pain also arose in his belly, and began in a most violent manner. . . . When he had been quite worn out by the pain in his belly for five days, he departed this life." Josephus, *Antiquities* 19.8.2.

him what rulers throughout history have longed to hear when they speak: "The voice of a god, and not of a man!"

But, of course, Herod *was* just a man—a man in rebellion against the Creator King and his anointed King. And so we see God's hand at work again, this time striking this man who dared to rob him of his glory.

> Immediately an angel of the Lord struck him down, because he did not give God the glory, and he was eaten by worms and breathed his last. (12:23)

How different is the death of King Herod from the death of King Jesus. Jesus was stretched out on the cross, the hand of God against him in judgment—not because he robbed God of glory but because you and I have done so. He was "smitten by God, and afflicted" (Isa. 53:4–5) so that we might be healed. King Jesus gave God glory even as he breathed his last. He was not eaten up by worms in death but was raised to life and has ascended to the right hand of the throne of God. Nothing and no one can thwart his plans for salvation and judgment. Nothing can stop his salvation message from spreading.

But the word of God increased and multiplied (12:24)

As we make our way through the book of Acts, we see again and again that the word of God is spreading and people are being saved. But we also see again and again that his witnesses are being opposed. There is suffering at every step of gospel advance.

Perhaps we should just admit that we don't like that this is so. We don't want it to be this way. In fact, there is a part of us that just doesn't understand why our sovereign God doesn't make this easier for his servants. We'd like it if the story of the word of God increasing and multiplying in the world was the story of a steady, unopposed, untroubled, unhindered, uncontroversial increase in the embrace of

Christ. But if we think that's what we should expect, we haven't been listening. Jesus made it clear: "A servant is not greater than his master. If they persecuted me, they will also persecute you" (John 15:20).

So what are we meant to take away from this account of the hand of God at work in this passage? How do we reckon with the reality that James is killed and Peter is rescued? There is a part of us that wants to say, "This is not the sort of salvation story we want. Besides, this doesn't seem fair." We can almost imagine James's mother, who was so ambitious for her sons, James and John, saying to Peter's mother, "Why did God rescue your son but not mine?"

We want to be able to find an answer to this question in this passage, just as we want to be able to find an answer to questions like these in our own circumstances. We don't know why some people recover and others don't, why some people suffer significantly for the gospel and others don't seem to. We'd like to know. But we don't.

So we lean into what we do know. And here's what we know. We know that God's plans for his gospel and for the ultimate salvation of his people are firmly in his hands. Nothing and no one can thwart them. Not a blood-thirsty mob. Not a power-hungry tyrant. Not a cancer-causing gene. Not a drunk driver. There is no promise in the Bible that God will always use his powerful hand to rescue his own from physical harm in this world. But his promise to save still stands. Jesus said, "I give them eternal life, and they will never perish, and no one will snatch them out of my hand. My Father, who has given them to me, is greater than all, and no one is able to snatch them out of the Father's hand" (John 10:28–29). My friends, we're in good hands.

Certainly Jesus believed that. As Jesus endured the cruelest of deaths, he said, "Father, into your hands I commit my spirit!" (Luke 23:46). If Jesus found the hands of his Father to be the safest of all places to be, we can too, no matter what happens to us in this life.

PART 3

SALVATION TO THE
ENDS OF THE EARTH

ASIA

CAPPADOCIA

Antioch
in Pisidia •

GALATIA

• Iconium

Lystra •

• Derbe

][Cilician Gates

LYCIA

• Tarsus

Attalia • • Perga

CILICIA

PAMPHYLIA

Seleucia • • Antioch

• Myra

SYRIA

• Salamis

CYPRUS

Paphos •

Damascus •

Mediterranean Sea

GALILEE

SAMARIA

Jerusalem ◇

JUDEA

10

All That God Had Done with Them

Acts 13:1–14:28   *Luke*

HAVE YOU EVER EXPRESSED appreciation to someone for something they have done for the kingdom, and their response was, "Oh, it wasn't me, it was the Lord"? Or have you ever been the person who said that? Why do we say that?

I think we're uncomfortable taking all the credit. We really do sense that the Spirit is the one who empowered and enabled us to do what he called us to do. But is there a sense in which, when someone shows appreciation for something we've done, we should just receive it? Didn't we do something?

There is some mystery in the way God accomplishes his work in the world through his people. We might like to be able to quantify it, to be able to say, "It was 50 percent him and 50 percent me," or even, "It was all God, not me." But the Bible won't let us do that. The Bible insists on two things being simultaneously true. God is the one who accomplishes the work of salvation. But what is also deeply true is that God has determined to accomplish his work of salvation through the strategy and the sacrifice, the proclamation, and the prayers of his people.

In the two chapters of Acts we're going to consider, Luke seems to want us to see what happens in this light. He seems to want us to see that God is working out his plans for salvation going to the ends of the earth. God is at work calling, judging, revealing, appointing, healing, and saving. And at the same time, Luke wants us to see how God is accomplishing this work. God is accomplishing his work of salvation through human sending, going, teaching, praying, and pleading. This is still the way that God accomplishes his work in the world, and because of that, we get to be a part of it! What a grace of our sovereign God, that he uses people like us to accomplish his saving work in the world.

Divine and Human Sending from Antioch

What we read in Acts 13 and 14 is usually called Paul's first missionary journey. Antioch has had years of careful Bible teaching, and now it will become the base of mission to take the gospel the next step toward the ends of the earth.

> Now there were in the church at Antioch prophets and teachers, Barnabas, Simeon who was called Niger, Lucius of Cyrene, Manaen a lifelong friend of Herod the tetrarch, and Saul. While they were worshiping the Lord and fasting, the Holy Spirit said, "Set apart for me Barnabas and Saul for the work to which I have called them." Then after fasting and praying they laid their hands on them and sent them off. So, being sent out by the Holy Spirit, they went down to Seleucia, and from there they sailed to Cyprus. (13:1–4)

Luke lists for us the names of the leaders of the church that has been established in Antioch. It is led by men from Africa, Cyprus, Judea and Samaria, and Asia Minor. Some are Jews; some are likely Gentiles. There's a Levite, a Pharisee, and one of Herod's close associates. They are worshiping and fasting, and in the midst of that, the Spirit speaks, instructing them to set apart Barnabas and Saul for the work of taking the gospel farther out. This is going to cost this church. It is going to cost them two-fifths of their pastoral staff. And certainly they're not sending these men off empty-handed. Likely this church is sending them with funds for the long journey ahead and with other tangible support they will need along the way. Everyone in the church is getting in on the sending.

But it is not just the church that is setting them apart and sending them off. They are "being sent out by the Holy Spirit" (v. 4). It is the Spirit who has called them, equipped them, and is at work in and through the church in Antioch to send them off. So there is both divine and human sending.

Divine Judgment and Human Teaching on Cyprus

Barnabas and Saul set off to fulfill a divine plan using human strategy. They're not simply setting sail and waiting to see where the winds blow them. They have a strategy for accomplishing God's divine plan. First, they go to the place Barnabas knows best, the island he's from, Cyprus, and they land in the coastal city of Salamis and begin to work their way across the island.

> When they arrived at Salamis, they proclaimed the word of God in the synagogues of the Jews. (13:5)

We're going to see that whenever Paul and his ministry companions arrive in a new city, their first stop is always the local synagogue. But notice that here in Salamis, "synagogues" is plural. This is a city where many Jews have settled and so there are numerous synagogues where Barnabas likely knows many people.

> When they had gone through the whole island as far as Paphos, they came upon a certain magician, a Jewish false prophet named Bar-Jesus. He was with the proconsul, Sergius Paulus, a man of

intelligence, who summoned Barnabas and Saul and sought to hear the word of God. (13:6–7)

Barnabas and Saul have worked their way from one side of Cyprus to the other, ending up in the capital city. There, they come upon a Jewish false prophet who has ingratiated himself with the Roman authority on the island with claims that he can provide divine knowledge. His name is Elymas, but he goes by Bar-Jesus, which means "son of Joshua" or "son of salvation." Perhaps his father's name is Joshua. Or perhaps he calls himself Bar-Jesus to make people think he has the power to bring salvation to those who are willing to listen to him. Saul is going to make it clear that Bar-Jesus is the furthest thing from being a "son of salvation." Sergius Paulus wants to hear the word of God, the word that brings salvation, and Bar-Jesus is out to do whatever it takes to keep that from happening.

But Elymas the magician (for that is the meaning of his name) opposed them, seeking to turn the proconsul away from the faith. But Saul, who was also called Paul, filled with the Holy Spirit, looked intently at him and said, "You son of the devil, you enemy of all righteousness, full of all deceit and villainy, will you not stop making crooked the straight paths of the Lord? And now, behold, the hand of the Lord is upon you, and you will be blind and unable to see the sun for a time." Immediately mist and darkness fell upon him, and he went about seeking people to lead him by the hand. (13:8–11)

This is the first time in the book that Saul is called by his Greek name, Paul, as he now has more interaction with Gentiles. Paul says that Bar-Jesus is not a "son of salvation" but is rather a "son of the devil" who does not want to open up the pathway to peace with God for Sergius Paulus. Rather, Elymas wants to make that straight path crooked, leading him astray. But instead of succeeding in leading Sergius astray, Elymas ends up in the dark himself, unable to lead anyone and needing help to find his way. So Elymas experiences the judgment of God, and Sergius Paulus experiences the salvation of God.

> Then the proconsul believed, when he saw what had occurred, for he was astonished at the teaching of the Lord. (13:12)

The divine miracle of judgment gave Paul and Barnabas's teaching credibility, confirming them as true spokesmen for God with a divine message. And as Sergius Paulus listened to what they had to say about Jesus, he was astonished! The gospel is astonishing, especially if you have never heard it before. God is at work through Paul and Barnabas, opening the door of faith to the Gentiles, and the most senior member of the government on the island of Cyprus has walked through that door.

Divine Revelation and Human Explanation at Antioch in Pisidia

Paul and Barnabas set sail for what we would know as modern-day Turkey and made their way to the next major city on their strategically planned route, Antioch in Pisidia (13:13–14). (Because there were sixteen cities named Antioch in the ancient world, ancient writers took care to distinguish them from one another.[1]) Once again they made their way to the synagogue where they waited for an opportunity to present their case to the Jews and the God-fearing Gentiles gathered there.

> After the reading from the Law and the Prophets, the rulers of the synagogue sent a message to them, saying, "Brothers, if you have any word of encouragement for the people, say it." (13:15)

From verses 17 to 41, Paul traces about two thousand years of the history of God's outworking of his salvation plans for his people. God led his people out of the land of Egypt and into the land of Canaan

---

1 Darrell L. Bock, *Acts*, Baker Exegetical Commentary on the New Testament (Grand Rapids, MI: Baker Academic, 2007), 450.

(13:17–19). He gave them judges (13:20). He gave them a king (13:21–22). Throughout their history—in deliverance, land, short-term saviors, and kings—he was showing them in shadow form the greater deliverance, the greater inheritance, the greater Savior and King he would send. And now Jesus, the substance that cast the shadows, has come!

> Of this man's offspring God has brought to Israel a Savior, Jesus, as he promised. (13:23)

But the way Jesus has accomplished salvation is not what the Jews expected. Jesus made salvation possible through his innocent death and his victorious resurrection. Paul goes on to explain that because the Jews "did not recognize him nor understand the utterances of the prophets, which are read every Sabbath, [they] fulfilled them by condemning him" (13:27). In verse 33 Paul says that Psalm 2:7, in which God says to his king, "You are my Son, today I have begotten you," is really about the establishment of Jesus as King. In verse 34 Paul says that in Jesus's ascension to David's thone, he was receiving the "holy and sure blessings of David," promised in Isaiah 55:3. In verse 35 he says that when David wrote in Psalm 16:10, "You will not let your Holy One see corruption," it was most profoundly about the resurrection of David's greater son, Jesus. Each of these Old Testament passages speaks of the resurrection, exaltation, and enthronement of God's king.

Paul's message was that the promise God made of a son of David who would be a King to reign over his people forever has been fulfilled in Jesus. The King is alive. And all the benefits of being a citizen of his kingdom are available to those who come under his kingship. I'm sure the history lesson was helpful, but I wonder if their hearts began to melt when Paul got to this:

> Let it be known to you therefore, brothers, that through this man forgiveness of sins is proclaimed to you, and by him everyone who

believes is freed from everything from which you could not be freed by the law of Moses. (13:38–39)

What good news—for them and for us! You and I can be freed from everything we could never be free from by simply trying harder to do the right thing yet failing again and again. Our debt for sin has been paid in full, and the righteousness of another—Jesus himself—has been credited to our account.

As good as this good news is, Paul knows that not everyone hearing it will receive it. And he wants to warn them of what rejecting this offer of salvation will mean for them. So he harkens back to the prophet Habakkuk, who wrote his book in a day when many were scoffing at the judgment God said was about to come upon Israel. Paul cites what God said through Habakkuk:

"Look, you scoffers,
    be astounded and perish;
for I am doing a work in your days,
    a work that you will not believe, even if one tells it to you."
    (13:41; cf. Hab. 1:5)

By quoting Habakkuk, Paul is issuing the same warning of coming judgment to the Jews in Antioch in Pisidia who scoff at the message of salvation and judgment.

Clearly this word of God's promises of salvation and judgment did a work in many of the Jews and God-fearing Gentiles who heard them that day. But as is the case everywhere Paul and Barnabas go, while some believe and are saved, others reject and oppose their message. The gospel divides. Many Jews wanted to hear more. But when Paul showed up on the next Sabbath and there were crowds of Gentiles there to hear his message, many of the Jews were filled with jealousy (13:45). They didn't like that the promises they thought of as being just for them were being offered to and embraced by Gentiles. Paul's way of responding to their opposition was to quote the prophet Isaiah:

> "For so the Lord has commanded us, saying,
>
> 'I have made you a light for the Gentiles,
>   that you may bring salvation to the ends of the earth.'"
>   (13:47; cf. Isa. 49:6)

This verse from Isaiah reveals the divine purpose that undergirds Paul's human effort: the salvation of God extending to the ends of the earth.

Divine Election and Human Belief at Antioch in Pisidia

Hearing Isaiah quoted at them may have made many of the Jews in the crowd even madder. But it clearly made the Gentiles happy.

> And when the Gentiles heard this, they began rejoicing and glorifying the word of the Lord, and as many as were appointed to eternal life believed. (13:48)

Here is the reason that Paul and Barnabas can keep on giving out a gospel that divides. They rest in divine election, which precedes human belief. When Paul and Barnabas share the gospel, they do so with passion and pleading. They give everything to it. And then they trust God with the results. They know that "as many as were appointed to eternal life" will believe and be saved. They know that God loves to save, but he doesn't save everyone.

> And the word of the Lord was spreading throughout the whole region. But the Jews incited the devout women of high standing and the leading men of the city, stirred up persecution against Paul and

Barnabas, and drove them out of their district. But they shook off the dust from their feet against them and went to Iconium. And the disciples were filled with joy and with the Holy Spirit. (13:49–52)

They trust God for who will respond in repentance and faith, and they trust God with those who reject their message as symbolized by shaking the dust from their feet as they depart Antioch Pisidia. Do you see how freeing this is?

While growing up, I was part of a youth ministry that impressed on me the importance of being a soul winner. And I'm so grateful for it. I learned the "Romans Road" so I could lead someone to Christ.[2] But what I was not given was an appropriate understanding of the role of human effort and proclamation under God's sovereignty. I felt like it was all up to me. It was all about my courage, my presentation, and my persistence. But salvation isn't up to me. "Salvation belongs to the Lord" (Jon. 2:9). It is our responsibility to proclaim the gospel of salvation, but it is God who saves. You and I don't know who he has appointed to eternal life. That means we should always be prepared and take the opportunities God gives us to share Christ. But we don't have to feel like failures when someone responds with apathy, indignation, or outright rejection. Paul and Barnabas rested in God's sovereignty, believing that he would use their gospel conversations to save some and harden others. And we should too.

Divine Wonders and Human Witness at Iconium

With the dust of Antioch Pisidia shaken from their feet, Paul and Barnabas move on to Iconium, an important commercial center of the Roman province of Galatia. In Iconium we see the same pattern of going to the Jews first at the synagogue, as well as the same division created there by the gospel message.

---

2   The "Romans Road" to salvation is a way of explaining the good news of salvation using verses from the book of Romans. It includes Rom. 3:23; 5:8; 6:23 and 5:1–2; 8:1; 10:9–10.

Now at Iconium they entered together into the Jewish synagogue and spoke in such a way that a great number of both Jews and Greeks believed. But the unbelieving Jews stirred up the Gentiles and poisoned their minds against the brothers. (14:1–2)

We might expect that this opposition would cause Paul and Barnabas to quickly move on. But it doesn't.

So they remained for a long time, speaking boldly for the Lord, who bore witness to the word of his grace, granting signs and wonders to be done by their hands. (14:3)

They are bold and persistent, speaking a word of grace to all who will listen. People are experiencing physical healing and wholeness accomplished by God through the hands of his servants. But the people in the city are divided (v. 4). Some are so bothered by this word of grace that they make plans to pelt Paul and Barnabas with rocks, the prescribed penalty for blasphemy (v. 5). But once again we discover God using persecution to simply spread his gospel in a place where the gospel needs to be heard. They "fled to Lystra and Derbe, cities of Lycaonia, and to the surrounding country, and there they continued to preach the gospel" (14:6).

Divine Miracle and a Human Plea at Lystra

In Lystra, Paul and Barnabas come upon a man who has been crippled since birth, and "seeing that he had faith to be made well" (14:9), Paul told him to stand on his feet and he "sprang up and began walking" (14:10).

And when the crowds saw what Paul had done, they lifted up their voices, saying in Lycaonian, "The gods have come down to us in the likeness of men!" Barnabas they called Zeus, and Paul, Hermes, because he was the chief speaker. And the priest of Zeus, whose temple was at the entrance to the city, brought oxen and garlands to the gates and wanted to offer sacrifice with the crowds. (14:11–13)

So often people think that if God will just do a miracle, then people will believe. But miracles don't always lead to genuine faith. They can lead to complete confusion. That is the case here.

The Lycaonians are confused. They're all familiar with a story told by the Roman poet Ovid. In this story, the Greek gods Zeus and Hermes assume human form and visit a town where one couple shows them hospitality while many in the town fail to show them hospitality. The couple who shows them hospitality are richly rewarded, while terrible judgment falls on those who did not.[3] Evidently, when the crowds in Lystra witnessed the miracle of a lame man being made able to walk, they assumed that Paul and Barnabas were Zeus and Hermes, and they wanted to make sure that appropriate hospitality was extended to them so they would be rewarded and not judged.

But, of course, Paul and Barnabas were horrified by their assumption that they were gods. These people had zero Old Testament background, so Paul was not going to preach to them using an Old Testament text as he did in his sermon to the Jews in Antioch of Pisidia. Instead, he draws upon something far more familiar to them, the text of creation.

But when the apostles Barnabas and Paul heard of it, they tore their garments and rushed out into the crowd, crying out, "Men, why are you doing these things? We also are men, of like nature with you, and we bring you good news, that you should turn from these vain things to a living God, who made the heaven and the earth and the sea and all that is in them. In past generations he allowed all the nations to

3   Apuleius, *Metamorphoses* 8.626–724.

walk in their own ways. Yet he did not leave himself without witness, for he did good by giving you rains from heaven and fruitful seasons, satisfying your hearts with food and gladness." (14:14–17)

We can, perhaps hear Paul saying, "The God who made heaven and earth has showered your life with all of the good things you enjoy. But none of these good things in this world can save you. They will all ultimately disappoint you. Turn from these vain things to a living God. There is a God, however, who did become human. His name is Jesus. He died and rose again from the dead. He will save you from a life of meaninglessness and false worship."

Crowds of Gentiles are listening to this sweet word of grace and mercy, and then:

Jews came from Antioch and Iconium, and having persuaded the crowds, they stoned Paul and dragged him out of the city, supposing that he was dead. But when the disciples gathered about him, he rose up and entered the city, and on the next day he went on with Barnabas to Derbe. (14:19–20)

The unbelieving Jews from the cities where Paul and Barnabas had been previously finally get the chance to throw stones at Paul. Imagine how badly injured he must have been for them to suppose that he was dead. Maybe he'll be quiet now. Maybe he'll go home now. Nope. The very next day he is up and on his way to the next city.

Divine Grace and Human Effort

We're given less than a verse on what happened in Derbe, but we're told that they "made many disciples" there (14:21). Paul has covered the major cities in the regions of Lycia and Galatia, and he is ready to go back to Antioch. We might assume that from Derbe, Paul and Barnabas would just take the short land-route home to Antioch. But their strategy is not about travel efficiencies; it's about presenting the gospel and then establishing churches in these key cities throughout Asia Minor that can become hubs themselves for sending out gospel messengers. So instead of taking the short land-route home, they retrace their steps, stopping at each of the cities throughout Asia Minor where they had made disciples and established churches. They stopped to encourage them for the difficulties ahead, to appoint elders to lead them, and to pray for them. And then:

> They sailed to Antioch, where they had been commended to the grace of God for the work that they had fulfilled. And when they arrived and gathered the church together, they declared all that God had done with them, and how he had opened a door of faith to the Gentiles. And they remained no little time with the disciples. (14:26–28)

It must have been good to be home and to have so much good news to share with all of those who had sacrificially supplied what they needed and sent them off for their year-long journey with the gospel. Those who supported them could rightly experience the joy of being a part of God's work through these messengers.

Notice that they had been commended to the grace of God for the work that *they had done* over the previous year in proclaiming the gospel of Christ. But what they want to declare is "all that *God had done* with them and how he had opened a door of faith to the Gentiles." This is the amazing thing about being a part of what God is doing in the world. It is genuine work. Hard work. We experience tremendous highs as people embrace and grow in Christ and their lives are changed. And we experience terrible lows of rejection and sometimes even being the target of mistreatment and harm. The joy of it is in knowing that somehow God is at work in and through our work.

My friends, as you do what God has called you to do, rest in knowing that God is sovereign over salvation and that he uses your proclamation of his gospel goodness to save some and harden others. Don't be discouraged when the gospel creates division. And when the task he has called you to and equipped you for is complete, expect to experience incredible joy over having been used by God himself to open the door of faith for someone else.

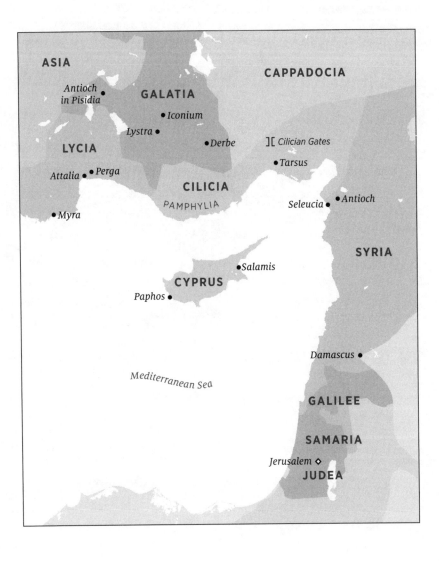

ASIA

CAPPADOCIA

Antioch
in Pisidia •

GALATIA

• Iconium

Lystra •

• Derbe

][Cilician Gates

• Tarsus

LYCIA

Attalia • • Perga

CILICIA

PAMPHYLIA

Seleucia •

• Antioch

• Myra

SYRIA

• Salamis

CYPRUS

Paphos •

Damascus •

Mediterranean Sea

GALILEE

SAMARIA

Jerusalem ◇

JUDEA

11

Saved through the Grace
of the Lord Jesus

Acts 15:1–16:5

I GREW UP IN THE CHURCH. My grandfather was a preacher and church planter. My dad was a deacon. I was at church on Sunday mornings, Sunday nights, Wednesday nights, for vacation Bible school in the summers, and often on Saturday when it was our turn to clean the building. I have great memories of being taught and being loved, of singing and serving. I also have memories of some really ugly conflicts.

I remember a Sunday when, in the midst of a big conflict with the leadership of the church, the pastor got up and simply read Numbers 16 in which Korah and his company assemble against Moses and Aaron. The story ends: "As soon as he had finished speaking all these words, the ground under them split apart. And the earth opened its mouth and swallowed them up, with their households and all the people who belonged to Korah and all their goods. So they and all that belonged to them went down alive into Sheol, and the earth closed over them, and they perished from the midst of the assembly" (Num. 16:31–33). And then the pastor shut his Bible and sat down. Message delivered.

I suppose wherever and whenever people are involved, there will be conflict. Some of us are conflict adverse. We want peace. We don't want to fight about anything. Others of us are always looking for something to be mad about, always itching for a fight.

Acts 14 ended with the good news that a door had been opened to the Gentiles. Everything seemed full steam ahead to take the gospel to the Gentiles who haven't yet heard it. But wait. There's a problem. How are Gentiles meant to walk through the door that has been opened to them? Can they get through the door if they don't become Jews first? That's the issue. And it is no small issue.

The Jerusalem church had heard the report from Peter of how the Spirit poured out on the Gentile Cornelius. The Antioch church had sent Paul and Barnabas to Asia Minor, and numerous churches had been planted. Larger numbers of Gentiles are entering in. But for some in the church in Jerusalem the response is, "Wait a minute. We're all for Gentiles coming in. We just want to make sure that they're coming in the right way." And the "right way," according to them, is that they become Jews first, with all that that means—circumcision, no eating pork, and getting to the temple in Jerusalem from time to time.

The leadership of the church in Antioch has not been making that requirement of the Gentiles who are coming to faith. So here is a potential conflict. But really it is more than that. It is going to create a sharp disagreement that threatens the continued spread of the gospel into the Gentile world.

A Disagreement That Threatens the Gospel Going to the World

Chapter 14 ended with Paul and Barnabas settling back into Antioch to stay for a while and serve the church after their first missionary journey.

> But some men came down from Judea and were teaching the brothers, "Unless you are circumcised according to the custom of Moses, you cannot be saved." (15:1)

We find out later that these men from the church in Jerusalem have come without the authorization of the Jerusalem church and their leadership (15:24). And what they are suggesting—that none of the Gentiles who are a part of their church are really saved if they haven't been circumcised—is, as you can imagine, troubling to the predominantly Gentile church in Antioch.

> And after Paul and Barnabas had no small dissension and debate with them, Paul and Barnabas and some of the others were appointed to go up to Jerusalem to the apostles and the elders about this question. (15:2)

Luke is tactful in the way he recounts this: there was no little debate. That's a nice way of saying that this was a big-time argument that created significant dissension in the Antioch church. This issue went to the heart of what it means to be a member of the new-covenant community, and more than that, what is required to be accepted by God. Imagine what the outcome of this disagreement would mean for all the Gentiles who had already taken hold of Jesus by faith, and what it would mean for how the gospel and its demands would be articulated to the ends of the earth going forward.

This issue was not going to be settled by the leaders of the church in Antioch and these Jerusalem church members who had shown up in Antioch with their demands. It was so important, so pivotal to the gospel going to the world, it would need to be taken up by the church in Jerusalem, which was led by the twelve apostles.

> So, being sent on their way by the church, they passed through both Phoenicia and Samaria, describing in detail the conversion of the Gentiles, and brought great joy to all the brothers. When they came to Jerusalem, they were welcomed by the church and the apostles and the elders, and they declared all that God had done with them. But some believers who belonged to the party of the Pharisees rose

up and said, "It is necessary to circumcise them and to order them to keep the law of Moses." (15:3–5)

Paul and Barnabas are in the middle of telling the church in Jerusalem all about what God had done through them in their journey to Cyprus and Pamphylia and Galatia, when some members of the church who had come to Christ out of the Pharisee party stood up to say, in essence, "Gentiles have to become Jews first to be saved." We remember that Pharisees are the guys who took commands in Exodus and Leviticus that were intended only for priests and imposed them on all Jews. They were big on cleansing rituals and Sabbath observance and fasting. While these particular Pharisees had embraced Christ, evidently the mindset of Pharisaism still had a hold on them. Sometimes it takes a while for the truths of the grace and mercy of Christ to work through new believers so that they are able to overcome instincts hewn over a lifetime, doesn't it?

The apostles and the elders were gathered together to consider this matter. And after there had been much debate, Peter stood up and said to them, "Brothers, you know that in the early days God made a choice among you, that by my mouth the Gentiles should hear the word of the gospel and believe." (15:6–7)

When Peter speaks about "the early days," he's referring to the time ten years earlier when the Spirit told him to go to the home of Cornelius in Caesarea, where the first large-scale Gentile conversion took place.

"And God, who knows the heart, bore witness to them, by giving them the Holy Spirit just as he did to us, and he made no distinction between us and them, having cleansed their hearts by faith." (15:8–9)

Circumcision was a rite of cleansing. Ever since Abraham was in-structed to be circumcised, circumcision had pointed to greater cleansing to come that would not only mark the body but also change the heart. What Peter witnessed in Caesarea was that the cleansing that circumcision had always pointed to that became a reality for Jewish believers when the Holy Spirit descended to dwell in them also became a reality in the Gentiles when the Holy Spirit descended on them. The same Spirit. The same cleansing. Hearts cleansed by faith. No physical circumcision required. Peter continues:

> "Now, therefore, why are you putting God to the test by placing a yoke on the neck of the disciples that neither our fathers nor we have been able to bear?" (15:10)

In what way is requiring circumcision putting God to the test? According to Brian Vickers, "to put God to the test is to know what God desires and requires but to decide nevertheless to go another way, or at least push the boundaries of what he requires."[1] In this case, to resist the reality of the transition from the old covenant to the new covenant by continuing to insist on physical circumcision was to put God to the test. Peter then points at the Mosaic law and perhaps looks into the eyes of those gathered in the room and asks why they would want to heave onto these Gentile converts the burden to try to live up to the demands of the law of Moses, when no Jew except for Jesus had ever been able to keep it.

> "But we believe that we will be saved through the grace of the Lord Jesus, just as they will." (15:11)

Notice that they are discussing the salvation of Gentiles, but Peter states how Jews are saved: through the grace of the Lord Jesus. Perhaps they needed to be reminded of this. After a lifetime defined by keeping

---

1 Brian J. Vickers, *John–Acts*, ESV Expository Commentary (Wheaton, IL: Crossway, 2019), 477.

the law of Moses, they probably needed frequent reminders that they were not saved through law-keeping, but have been saved by grace. And Gentiles are saved the same way: through the grace of the Lord Jesus. Keeping the law can't save anyone. Only the grace of Jesus can save. And it can save anyone.

> And all the assembly fell silent, and they listened to Barnabas and Paul as they related what signs and wonders God had done through them among the Gentiles. (15:12)

Peter finishes, and nobody says anything. Perhaps they're thinking it through. Clearly they have no good argument to make against what Peter has presented. Barnabas and Paul then add to their case, recounting how God had accomplished signs and wonders through them among the Gentiles and perhaps, by implication, indicating that no circumcision was required by God among the Gentiles to receive the healings and miracles they performed.

Peter has spoken. Now it is James's turn to speak. James, the half-brother of Jesus, has become the leader in the Jerusalem church.

> After they finished speaking, James replied, "Brothers, listen to me. Simeon has related how God first visited the Gentiles, to take from them a people for his name. And with this the words of the prophets agree, just as it is written,
>
>> 'After this I will return,
>> and I will rebuild the tent of David that has fallen;
>> I will rebuild its ruins,
>>   and I will restore it.'" (15:13–16)

James quotes the prophet Amos, who, long after the kingdom split into a northern kingdom and a southern kingdom, foretold of a day when Yahweh would restore the Davidic kingdom. At Pentecost, when the Spirit was poured on the Jews gathered in Jerusalem—Jews from both the northern and southern kingdoms—the restoration God promised through Amos was fulfilled. But that was not all Amos had to say. He continued by giving the purpose for this restoration, which James quotes:

> ". . . that the remnant of mankind may seek the Lord,
>   and all the Gentiles who are called by my name,
>   says the Lord, who makes these things known from of old."
>   (15:17–18)

The purpose of the restoration of the kingdom was so that "the remnant of mankind," all of the peoples of the world who are not Israelites, would seek the Lord and be called by his name. James is using the words of Amos to say that Gentiles coming into the people of God as Gentiles had always been God's plan. Indeed, all of God's dealings with Israel throughout history had been leading up to this great climax: the Son of David seated on the throne over a regathered, restored Israel joined by people of every nation who belong to him.

James doesn't want to put any barriers in front of "all the Gentiles who are called by [the Lord's] name." He doesn't want to place a burden of Mosaic law-keeping on them. But he does think there are some things that the Gentiles who are turning away from pagan idolatry and toward Christ need to do.

> "Therefore my judgment is that we should not trouble those of the
> Gentiles who turn to God, but should write to them to abstain from
> the things polluted by idols, and from sexual immorality, and from
> what has been strangled, and from blood." (15:19–20)

Throughout much of the Roman Empire, most meat made its way onto people's plates after having been offered to an idol. James is saying that Gentile believers should avoid eating meat that comes to them in that way. Similarly, sexual immorality was a part of pagan worship and a pagan lifestyle. Sexual chastity represented an entirely new way of life for Gentile believers. James says they must pursue it. The meat of an animal slaughtered by strangulation would not have been properly drained of blood. Abstaining from these things will be a way of making an absolute break with their old life of pagan idolatry. Abstaining from these things will also accomplish something else: it will remove unnecessary offense toward Jews so that these Gentile believers can effectively evangelize unbelieving Jews and find unity with believing Jews.

> "For from ancient generations Moses has had in every city those who proclaim him, for he is read every Sabbath in the synagogues." (15:21)

James is saying that throughout the Gentile world, Jews are hearing the law read every week in the synagogues. These Jews simply won't be able to hear the gospel from someone who eats meat sacrificed to idols, eats meat with the blood in it, or drinks the blood of an animal. James is clear that Gentiles are not saved by avoiding these things. Avoiding these things provides tangible evidence of their turn away from idolatry and their desire to see Christ's kingdom increase. It is love for lost Jews that James says should compel them to abstain.

Evidently Peter, Paul, Barnabas, and James were convincing in their arguments. Luke writes that "it seemed good to the apostles and the elders, with the whole church, to choose men from among them and send them to Antioch with Paul and Barnabas" (15:22). They were sent back to Antioch with a letter that spelled out their decision for the church in Antioch:

> "For it has seemed good to the Holy Spirit and to us to lay on you no greater burden than these requirements: that you abstain from

what has been sacrificed to idols, and from blood, and from what has been strangled, and from sexual immorality. If you keep yourselves from these, you will do well. Farewell." (15:28–29)

This is one of the most important letters in history.[2] The believers back in Antioch already knew that Paul and Barnabas were opposed to the demands of the Pharisees, but this letter let them know that a more formal decision had been made by the apostolic leaders of the new-covenant community in Jerusalem.

This letter clarified the gospel. Nothing is to be added to salvation, which is by grace alone through faith alone. It demonstrated the church's unequivocal commitment to the purity of the gospel that it is taking to the nations.

So when they were sent off, they went down to Antioch, and having gathered the congregation together, they delivered the letter. And when they had read it, they rejoiced because of its encouragement. And Judas and Silas, who were themselves prophets, encouraged and strengthened the brothers with many words. And after they had spent some time, they were sent off in peace by the brothers to those who had sent them. But Paul and Barnabas remained in Antioch, teaching and preaching the word of the Lord, with many others also. (15:30–35)

Notice the impact of the letter and those who delivered it to the church in Antioch. It made them happy! (I imagine happiness mixed with relief!) It encouraged them in the gospel, impressing the pure gospel a little deeper into their hearts and minds. Their grip on the true

---

2   According to Guy Prentiss Waters, "In saying that 'it seemed good to the Holy Spirit and to us,' the Council is claiming neither divine inspiration nor infallibility for its decision. On the contrary, it is declaring its persuasion that its decision is agreeable to the mind of the Spirit; that is, to the mind of Christ who has poured out his Spirit upon the church." *A Study Commentary on the Acts of the Apostles* (Louisville, KY: Evangelical Press, 2015), 367.

gospel got a little tighter. Lingering tethers to their old life of idolatry were severed.

What began with a sharp disagreement, a disagreement that threatened the gospel going to the world, ended with the strengthening of those who worked through it and the clarity wrought by it. It was a disagreement about something critical, something essential, something foundational. But there are some disagreements that arise amongst those in the church that really aren't so critical, disagreements that don't threaten the gospel making progress in the world. And that is what we read about next.

A Disagreement That Doesn't Threaten the Gospel Going to the World

Verse 35 ended the previous section with the report that Paul and Barnabas remained in Antioch teaching and preaching. But after a while Paul was ready to visit all of the churches they had planted on their first missionary journey.

> And after some days Paul said to Barnabas, "Let us return and visit the brothers in every city where we proclaimed the word of the Lord, and see how they are." Now Barnabas wanted to take with them John called Mark. But Paul thought best not to take with them one who had withdrawn from them in Pamphylia and had not gone with them to the work. And there arose a sharp disagreement. (15:36–39a)

Here's my summary of what happened:

Paul: "Let's go back to every city where we've proclaimed the gospel and see how they're doing."

Barnabas: "Great. Let's take John Mark with us."

Paul: "Nope. He didn't complete the trip last time we took him with us."

To Paul, John Mark's departure from their team early on in their first missionary journey was a defection, and he's not up for risking that again. To Barnabas, the "son of encouragement," his nephew John Mark is someone worthy of a second chance. Luke says they had a "sharp disagreement." But this isn't a disagreement that threatens the gospel going to the world. It's not a gospel issue at stake; it's a wisdom issue, one that two men who are filled with the Spirit see differently. They're unified in their mission but divided on how best to go about accomplishing it.

So . . . they separated from each other. Barnabas took Mark with him and sailed away to Cyprus, but Paul chose Silas and departed, having been commended by the brothers to the grace of the Lord. And he went through Syria and Cilicia, strengthening the churches. (15:39b–41)

I have to imagine this was not only a sharp dispute; it must also have been a painful dispute. Think about all that Paul and Barnabas had accomplished together, the opposition they had endured together, the highs and lows they had uniquely shared with each other. It must have been painful to part ways. Sometimes two Spirit-filled people can see things differently and determine that wisdom is separating, with each continuing to pursue the mission. Here, at least, the mission was not hindered, but expanded.

The result of working through their disagreement and going different directions not only didn't threaten the gospel going out to the world but actually strengthened it. Originally Paul and Barnabas were a group of two. Now they split and each has a new partner, so the group of two has expanded to two groups of two. They're unified in their mission while divided on the specific staffing for the mission. And the result was that they covered more ground with the gospel.

A Decision That Serves the Gospel Going to the World

So far we've witnessed two disagreements: one that threatened and one that did not threaten gospel progress to the ends of the earth. As we enter into chapter 16, we read about a decision that serves gospel progress.

Paul and Silas headed out from Antioch and eventually arrived in Lystra, where Paul had been stoned nearly to death the last time he was there. Perhaps you or I might like to avoid this city, but Paul wants to strengthen the church that he planted there, so he's not avoiding it.

> A disciple was there, named Timothy, the son of a Jewish woman who was a believer, but his father was a Greek. He was well spoken of by the brothers at Lystra and Iconium. Paul wanted Timothy to accompany him. (16:1–3a)

Paul wants Timothy to accompany him as they seek to cover more ground for the gospel, but first they have to have a conversation. Because Timothy's father was Greek, Jews would assume that Timothy had not been circumcised. And they would be right. Maybe Timothy and Paul's conversation went something like this:

> Timothy: "I love hearing about the contents of the letter the Jerusalem church sent to Antioch. Isn't it wonderful news? No one ever needs to be circumcised again!"

> Paul: "Uh, yes, it's wonderful. No one ever . . . except you."

> Timothy: "Excuse me?"

> Paul: "Timothy, you don't have to be circumcised to be saved, but I'd like for you to be circumcised so that the Jews in the synagogues where we're going will listen to what you have to say about Jesus."

What will Timothy say? This is a big ask.

> Timothy: "I'll do it. The advance of the gospel matters that much to me."

These two chapters together tell us that if someone is demanding circumcision as a prerequisite to salvation, Paul will stand firm against it. But if circumcision will enhance the possibility of a hearing for the gospel, he's all for it.

> And he took him and circumcised him because of the Jews who were in those places, for they all knew that his father was a Greek. As they went on their way through the cities, they delivered to them for observance the decisions that had been reached by the apostles and elders who were in Jerusalem. So the churches were strengthened in the faith, and they increased in numbers daily. (16:3b–5)

We read that as they go, they are communicating the decision regarding Gentiles not needing to become Jews and that this message is strengthening these churches in the faith. They're made stronger by the clarity of the decision on how a person is saved: not by becoming a Jew but by receiving the grace of Jesus to repent and believe.

The two disagreements and the decision in this passage show us something important: we don't have to be afraid of disagreements in the church. Disagreements can actually help us to clarify the gospel. Disagreements rightly handled can lead to strengthening of the church rather than division in the church. And some disagreements matter more than others.

Last I checked, that church I grew up in, where the pastor read about the rebels against Moses being swallowed up by the ground, is still there. Nobody has been swallowed up. Over my lifetime, I've witnessed a whole lot more disagreements in the church—things worthy of being argued about and things that aren't. In fact, I sometimes feel that there is more dissension and debate in the church than ever. So what do we do?

I think I know what Paul would say. It's what he will write to the church in Ephesus about twelve years after this conflict:

> I therefore, a prisoner for the Lord, urge you to walk in a manner worthy of the calling to which you have been called, with all humility and gentleness, with patience, bearing with one another in love, eager to maintain the unity of the Spirit in the bond of peace. (Eph. 4:1–3)

Let's be wise in evaluating disagreements in the church. Disagreements about what is at the heart of saving faith really matter. We simply can't lock arms with those who don't hold to salvation by grace alone through faith alone in the finished work of Christ alone. But disagreements about secondary issues or methods are different. While disagreements about strategy and methods do matter and might lead to pursuing the mission separately, they are not cause for disfellowship or disdain. Depending on the issue, we may decide we can cooperate together in certain aspects of ministry, or we might decide we simply can't work together in good conscience. But that doesn't mean we don't still consider them brothers and sisters in Christ and fellow servants of the same Lord.

Rather than being quick to criticize, quick to stoke the fires of conflict, let's be eager to maintain the unity of the Spirit in the bond of peace. Let's be people who are not only saved by the grace of the Lord Jesus but people who are consistent conduits of that grace, even to, perhaps especially to, those we disagree with.

MOESIA

DALMATIA

THRACE

Black Sea

MACEDONIA

Thessalonica•   • Philippi

EPIRUS

SAMOTHRACE

BITHYNIA

GALATIA

CAPPADOCIA

Troas•
•Assos   MYSIA

Mitylene•

ASIA   Antioch
in Pisidia

Thyatira

•Athens   • Ephesus   •Iconium

Corinth•   •Miletus   Lystra•   •Derbe

ACHAIA   •Tarsus

LYCIA   CILICIA   •Antioch

RHODES   •Patara   SYRIA

CRETE   Mediterranean Sea   CYPRUS

•Gortyna   •Damascus

Tyre•
•Ptolemais

Caesarea•   PALESTINE

Jerusalem•

Via Egnatia
•Philippi

Pella   •Neapolis

Amphipolis•

Thessalonica•

Berea•   Apollonia

12

There Is Another King, Jesus

Acts 16:6–17:9

I LIVED IN OLATHE, KANSAS, for most of my growing-up years. Our house on South Stevenson was about 1 mile away from I-35, the interstate highway that runs north and south across the country from Duluth, Minnesota, to Laredo, Texas. When David and I got married in Waco, Texas, we bought our first house on Seminole Trail, which was 2.2 miles from I-35. Later we moved to Coppell, Texas, where our house on Leisure Lane was less than 4 miles from I-35. Whenever I'm in a city and we get on I-35, whether it's Minneapolis or Des Moines or Oklahoma City or San Antonio, I always think, "I could get on this road and keep driving and get to some of the most significant places in my life."

I suppose most of us take modern roadways for granted. They're just there, and we resent the fact that road repair sometimes slows us down. But if we had lived in the first century, we would not have taken roads for granted.

It was in the third century BC that Rome began to expand outside the Italian Peninsula. One key to their expansion was the extensive road system they built through the ancient Mediterranean world, which made travel between major cities far more doable and direct than ever before. Built originally as avenues for Roman conquest and administration, it was the roads built by Rome that made it possible for Paul and his companions to travel to the many cities included in his missionary journeys recorded in Acts. In Acts 16 and 17 we get to walk with Paul on one of these Roman roads, the Via Egnatia, which runs from the coast of the Adriatic Sea in modern Albania all the way east to modern Istanbul.[1] It is going to take us to all of the significant places in these chapters. It had been built to support the invasion of the Roman Empire east into Macedonia and Asia. But in these chapters, we're going to witness a reverse invasion. Paul and Silas are headed west on this road. They're taking the gospel of another kingdom and another King into the Roman world ruled by Caesar. And there is sure to be a clash of kingdoms.

King Jesus Directs the Mission

As we pick up the story in Acts 16:6, Paul and Silas have departed Lystra with Timothy, and they have a plan in mind for where they want to take the gospel from there. It may be helpful to look at a map of the region in Paul's day to get a sense of their plan. Their plan was to depart from Lystra, in the center of Galatia, and work their way west through Asia toward Ephesus. But evidently, that wasn't God's plan.

> And they went through the region of Phrygia and Galatia, having been forbidden by the Holy Spirit to speak the word in Asia. (16:6)

---

1 According to the Via Egnatia Foundation, one can hike the Via Egnatia even today. Their website says, "Through mountains and valleys, along riverbeds, past lakes and seaside, villages and cities, the ancient Via Egnatia route goes 1000 km eastward to Istanbul. Parts of the old road have survived and are still there to enjoy for the observant hiker. It starts at Durrës on the Adriatic coast through Albania, Northern Macedonia and Greece and ending at Thessaloniki. A complete hiking guide is available at https://www.viaegnatiafoundation.eu/index.php/ve-on-foot-part-1/ve -on-foot" (accessed November 9, 2023). Anybody keen to go hiking with me?

We don't know how they determined that it had been forbidden by the Holy Spirit. Perhaps the Spirit spoke to them directly, or perhaps it was a less direct and yet unmistakable sense of what the Spirit desired. Or perhaps it was a matter of circumstances processed in light of God's sovereignty that prevented travel into that region.[2] Whichever it was, they changed course and headed northwest from Lystra toward the region north of Asia, Bithynia.

> And when they had come up to Mysia, they attempted to go into Bithynia, but the Spirit of Jesus did not allow them. (16:7)

Once again, their plan was thwarted. Interestingly, this time the text says they were not allowed to go there because the "Spirit of Jesus" did not allow them. Evidently Luke wants to press the point that King Jesus is the one directing the course of the spread of his gospel into the kingdoms of the world.

> So, passing by Mysia, they went down to Troas. And a vision appeared to Paul in the night: a man of Macedonia was standing there, urging him and saying, "Come over to Macedonia and help us." And when Paul had seen the vision, immediately we sought to go on into Macedonia, concluding that God had called us to preach the gospel to them. (16:8–10)

What a compelling vision this must have been for Paul—someone from a place that was not on their planned itinerary saying, "Come . . . help us." I wonder if Paul heard pleading in his voice or saw desperation in his eyes. What mattered most was that he knew that this wasn't just

---

2   Just because Paul and Silas were forbidden to take the gospel into Asia and Bithynia at that point in time didn't mean the gospel would never go into these areas, or even that they wouldn't take the gospel into these regions at a later date. Indeed, we're going to read about Paul taking the gospel to Ephesus in Asia. Just not yet.

a person bidding him to come, but God calling him to go. Paul awoke with fresh clarity for where they would head next with the gospel, and with fresh passion to provide the help he knew the Macedonians—indeed all people—need more than anything.

King Jesus Opens Hearts to His Gospel

> So, setting sail from Troas, we made a direct voyage to Samothrace, and the following day to Neapolis, and from there to Philippi, which is a leading city of the district of Macedonia and a Roman colony. (16:11–12a)

In Neapolis (present-day Kavala in northern Greece), they connected to and started down the Via Egnatia, the major east-west artery running through the heart of Macedonia. They would have traveled along the Via Egnatia for about 10 miles when they arrived in Philippi, which was a Roman colony. This means it was a miniature Rome, where the worship of Roman gods and worship of the emperor, Caesar, as lord and god was a way of life.

> We remained in this city some days. And on the Sabbath day we went outside the gate to the riverside, where we supposed there was a place of prayer, and we sat down and spoke to the women who had come together. (16:12b–13)

Paul's custom whenever he came to a new city was to first go to the synagogue, but evidently there was no synagogue to go to in this city. So they went to a place out by the Gangites River where some women assembled on the Sabbath to go through the appointed prayers.

> One who heard us was a woman named Lydia, from the city of Thyatira, a seller of purple goods, who was a worshiper of God. The Lord opened her heart to pay attention to what was said by Paul.

And after she was baptized, and her household as well, she urged us, saying, "If you have judged me to be faithful to the Lord, come to my house and stay." And she prevailed upon us. (16:14–15)

By the fact that she was a seller of purple goods, which were expensive in that day,[3] and that she had a house big enough to house this mission team of four,[4] we can assume that Lydia was wealthy. There were laws about who could deal in purple fabric, the fabric of royalty, so she likely had some connection to Caesar's household to be in this business. By the fact that Lydia was from Thyatira (interestingly, a city in Asia where Paul was forbidden by the Spirit to go), and that she is described as "a worshiper of God," we can assume that Lydia was a God-fearing Gentile. This means that she had at least some understanding of God's saving intentions for his people. But she didn't have the full picture. If she had some familiarity with the Jewish scriptures, she knew about the promise God made to David, that one of his sons would sit on his throne forever (2 Sam. 7:16). But she didn't know that Jesus, his Son, had come. This is at the heart of the "help" Paul has been summoned to give to the Macedonians.

As Lydia went to the riverside that day, she didn't know that something supernatural was about to happen to her. Indeed, what happened to her is what must happen to anyone and everyone who becomes a Christian: Jesus, the Lord, opened her heart. As Paul spoke, Jesus opened the heart of Lydia to make her receptive to the truth of the gospel. She wants to bow to this king. She wants everyone in her family and household to bow to him too. She wants her home to become

---

3 "Purple cloth was prized in the ancient world and was very expensive and time consuming to produce. The process involved boiling loads of a particular kind of sea snail that itself was not purple but when boiled produced chemicals that could be made into purple dyes." Brian J. Vickers, *John–Acts*, ESV Expository Commentary (Wheaton, IL: Crossway, 2019), 493.

4 In verse 10, Luke writes that God had called "us" to preach the gospel, and in verse 11 that "we" made a direct voyage. Evidently, Paul's team has increased to four as Luke himself has joined Paul, Silas, and Timothy.

an outpost of this kingdom, so she invites Paul's whole team to stay at her house. Evidently, she won't take no for an answer. King Jesus has opened her heart to the gospel, and in this way the kingdom of Jesus has invaded the Roman colony of Philippi.

King Jesus Binds the Strong Man

Evidently Paul and his companions continued to go out to the place of prayer by the river on the Sabbath, and perhaps at other times.

> As we were going to the place of prayer, we were met by a slave girl who had a spirit of divination and brought her owners much gain by fortune-telling. She followed Paul and us, crying out, "These men are servants of the Most High God, who proclaim to you the way of salvation." And this she kept doing for many days. (16:16–18a)

The scene reminds us of the numerous times in the Gospels when Jesus encountered people inhabited by demons who recognized who he was and the mission he was on to destroy the works of the devil (Luke 4:31–35; 8:27–33; 1 John 3:8; Rev. 20:10). In one of those situations he had said, "If it is by the Spirit of God that I cast out demons, then the kingdom of God has come upon you. Or how can someone enter a strong man's house and plunder his goods, unless he first binds the strong man? Then indeed he may plunder his house" (Matt. 12:28–29). Evidently "the strong man," Satan, is at work in Philippi too. The slave girl has come under his power.[5] But Jesus is about to plunder the strong man's house.

---

5   We might wonder how this young girl became a slave. Perhaps she was born to slaves. Or perhaps she was one of the millions of unwanted baby girls left to die outside the city, and someone saved her for the purpose of enslaving her. The ESV translates Acts 16:16 to say she had "a spirit of divination." The Greek indicates that she had a "python" spirit, or the Spirit of Pythia. According to Greek myth, Pythia was a priestess who was enabled to predict the future after inhaling the fumes of a python who was said to have been killed by the god Apollo. Rachel Lockett, "The Oracle of Delphi: The Ancient Greek Fortuneteller," *History Cooperative*, July 6, 2022, https://

Paul, having become greatly annoyed, turned and said to the spirit, "I command you in the name of Jesus Christ to come out of her." And it came out that very hour. (16:18b)

While the kingdom of Satan has been granted a great deal of power by God, it is completely under his authority. Jesus Christ is seated at the right hand of God, exercising his authority over evil. Paul merely commands the demon to come out of this girl in the name of Jesus, and it is done. Because King Jesus has bound the strong man, this little girl was freed from slavery to his evil.

But when her owners saw that their hope of gain was gone, they seized Paul and Silas and dragged them into the marketplace before the rulers. And when they had brought them to the magistrates, they said, "These men are Jews, and they are disturbing our city. They advocate customs that are not lawful for us as Romans to accept or practice." (16:19–21)

While Luke tells us her owners were driven by fear of losing income, they don't mention anything about that in their complaint to the magistrates. Their complaint is that Paul and his companions are disturbing the city. The Romans highly valued public order. Rome was generally tolerant when it came to religious matters, as long as those of other religions were not suspected of disturbing the peace, i.e., the peace of Rome, or the Pax Romana. They're accusing Paul and Silas of seeking to subvert the Roman way of life. Paul and Silas were advocating customs that had nothing to do with being devoted to the god Apollo but had everything to do with the grace of Jesus.

The crowd joined in attacking them, and the magistrates tore the garments off them and gave orders to beat them with rods. (16:22)

---

historycooperative.org/. Perhaps this little girl had been taken to the shrine of Apollo to inhale the fumes of the python so that she might have the capacity to predict the future.

Evidently the owners of the slave girl found it easy to persuade the crowd that had gathered to support their cause. It became such a disturbance that the city magistrates had to deal with it. The magistrates had attendants called lictors who carried a bundle of rods the size of a broomstick as an instrument to inflict punishment on the spot whenever someone was judged guilty.

> And when they had inflicted many blows upon them, they threw them into prison, ordering the jailer to keep them safely. Having received this order, he put them into the inner prison and fastened their feet in the stocks. (16:23–24)

Their backs flayed from the beating, Paul and Silas were taken to the innermost part of the prison where their feet were fastened into stocks. Likely the stocks were adjusted outward to the point of being just shy of pulling their legs out of joint.

> About midnight Paul and Silas were praying and singing hymns to God, and the prisoners were listening to them. (16:25)

I wonder what they were singing at midnight. What do you sing in the middle of the night when you're in that much pain? I wonder if they picked the longest psalm in the book, Psalm 119, and began to work their way through all of the verses to try to keep their minds off the physical agony. And if so, did they come to this verse?

> Though the cords of the wicked ensnare me,
>   I do not forget your law.
> At midnight I rise to praise you,
>   because of your righteous rules. (Ps. 119:61–62)

Perhaps it was right at midnight when:

Suddenly there was a great earthquake, so that the foundations of the prison were shaken. And immediately all the doors were opened, and everyone's bonds were unfastened. When the jailer woke and saw that the prison doors were open, he drew his sword and was about to kill himself, supposing that the prisoners had escaped. (16:26–27)

We might expect Paul and Silas to walk out of prison once their feet are no longer in stocks and the doors have swung open. That's certainly what the jailer expected when he was awakened by the earthquake. In fact, he was so sure they'd be gone that he didn't even check to see if they were still there. If his prisoners were gone, he would be a goner himself. He's so sure of it that he's not going to wait for the Roman authorities to execute him. He'll take care of it himself.

King Jesus Saves the Hopeless

But his prisoners are not gone. Paul and Silas have come to Macedonia to help. They're not out to preserve themselves; they're there to help the hopeless. They're there to give the good news to those who have never heard it. This jailer is hopeless and has never heard it.

But Paul cried with a loud voice, "Do not harm yourself, for we are all here." And the jailer called for lights and rushed in, and trembling with fear he fell down before Paul and Silas. Then he brought them out and said, "Sirs, what must I do to be saved?" (16:28–30)

How many times have you wished that someone would ask you a question like this: "What must I do to be saved?" But this jailer may not be thinking about salvation in the terms Paul and Silas and you and I do. Perhaps he's asking, "What do I have to do so that the Roman authorities don't kill me? What do I have to do to keep you from leaving? Do you want money? Do you want my house? Do you want me to become your slave?" This man is accustomed to operating in a ruthless kingdom. But Paul and Silas use the opportunity to introduce him to a grace-filled kingdom. If the jailor falls guilty before the Roman authorities, he'll die. But if he falls guilty before King Jesus, he will live.

> And they said, "Believe in the Lord Jesus, and you will be saved, you and your household." And they spoke the word of the Lord to him and to all who were in his house. And he took them the same hour of the night and washed their wounds; and he was baptized at once, he and all his family. Then he brought them up into his house and set food before them. And he rejoiced along with his entire household that he had believed in God. But when it was day, the magistrates sent the police, saying, "Let those men go." And the jailer reported these words to Paul, saying, "The magistrates have sent to let you go. Therefore come out now and go in peace." (16:31–36)

Maybe the magistrates thought the earthquake in the middle of the night was a message from their gods to get rid of these guys. Or maybe they thought Paul and Silas had been punished enough. Whatever their reason, Paul's not going to make it easy to get rid of them.

> But Paul said to them, "They have beaten us publicly, uncondemned, men who are Roman citizens, and have thrown us into prison; and do they now throw us out secretly? No! Let them come themselves and take us out." The police reported these words to the magistrates, and they were afraid when they heard that they were Roman citizens. So they came and apologized to them. And they took them out and asked them to leave the city. (16:37–39)

It seems that Paul and Silas might have mentioned the fact that they were Roman citizens back when those lictors lifted their rods to beat into their backs, doesn't it? Why didn't they? And why do Paul and

Silas insist that the magistrate come to the prison to personally walk them out?

Paul and Silas have in mind the progress of the gospel in Philippi. A small band of believers has come together in the city, and they want to do what they can to protect them from being treated harshly the way they've just been treated harshly. Paul wants the new believers to be heard as they continue to spread the gospel, and so he wants it to be clear that they had been falsely accused and therefore pardoned. He wants the city to know that Christians are not law breakers. Perhaps their public release will cause the magistrates to be slower to inflict harm on the new believers in the city if and when conflict arises in the future.

> So they went out of the prison and visited Lydia. And when they had seen the brothers, they encouraged them and departed. (16:40)

King Jesus Subverts Human Kingdoms

Asked to leave Philippi, Paul, Silas, and Timothy oblige, leaving behind a young house church.[6] They continue their journey along the Via Egnatia, passing through Amphipolis and Apollonia until they reach Thessalonica, the seat of provincial administration. Unlike Philippi, there was a sizeable number of Jews in this city and therefore it had a synagogue, which Paul and his friends attend on three successive sabbaths. Perhaps the Jews in Thessalonica knew that Paul had studied under the respected rabbi Gamaliel and so invited him to speak at their gathering. As he opened the scrolls, Paul argues that the Old Testament

---

6   We read later in his letter to the church in Philippi: "When I left Macedonia, no church entered into partnership with me in giving and receiving, except you only. Even in Thessalonica you sent me help for my needs once and again" (Phil. 4:15–16). On two occasions, within a few weeks of his departure, the church will send him gifts in the next major city along the Via Egnatia. Luke may have been left behind in Philippi, as the account is no longer written in terms of what "we" did. He may be the "true companion" Paul refers to in Philippians 4:3 whom he urges to help Syntyche and Euodia to "agree in the Lord" (vv. 2–3).

scriptures present a suffering Messiah who would come and that indeed this Messiah had come in the person of Jesus.

> "This Jesus, whom I proclaim to you, is the Christ." And some of them were persuaded and joined Paul and Silas, as did a great many of the devout Greeks and not a few of the leading women. But the Jews were jealous, and taking some wicked men of the rabble, they formed a mob, set the city in an uproar, and attacked the house of Jason, seeking to bring them out to the crowd. And when they could not find them, they dragged Jason and some of the brothers before the city authorities, shouting, "These men who have turned the world upside down have come here also, and Jason has received them, and they are all acting against the decrees of Caesar, saying that there is another king, Jesus." (17:3–7)

Those who opposed them have gotten the message. And they don't like it. Yes, there is another king, Jesus! Yes, Paul and Silas have come to turn a world in which people merely live for themselves and for the state upside down. They've come to turn a world in which the powerful oppress the weak and the rich oppress the poor upside down. They've come to plant outposts of the kingdom of heaven right inside the cities of the empire of Rome. They've come to turn upside down a world in which Caesar is worshiped as lord and savior because they know he is not Lord and he cannot save. Indeed, they have come with the good news that there is another king, Jesus.

My friends, King Jesus is nothing like Caesar. He is not a human king who claims to be a god. He is a king who is God and emptied himself of those privileges to become human. In fact, Paul will write to the church he has left behind in Macedonia:

> Have this mind among yourselves, which is yours in Christ Jesus, who, though he was in the form of God, did not count equality with

God a thing to be grasped, but emptied himself, by taking the form of a servant, being born in the likeness of men. And being found in human form, he humbled himself by becoming obedient to the point of death, even death on a cross. Therefore God has highly exalted him and bestowed on him the name that is above every name, so that at the name of Jesus every knee should bow, in heaven and on earth and under the earth, and every tongue confess that Jesus Christ is Lord, to the glory of God the Father. (Phil. 2:5–11)

When I really think about these words, "There is another king, Jesus," I realize that they are words I really need to hear too. In so many ways my life is about my little kingdom where I am sovereign. I have a set of priorities and preferences, and there is a part of me that doesn't like it so much when the word of God seems to want to turn things upside down. What we really need is for the kingdom of Jesus to turn so many more things in our own personal kingdoms upside down. We need to hear and submit to his decrees. We, too, need another king, a better king, to rule over our lives: King Jesus.

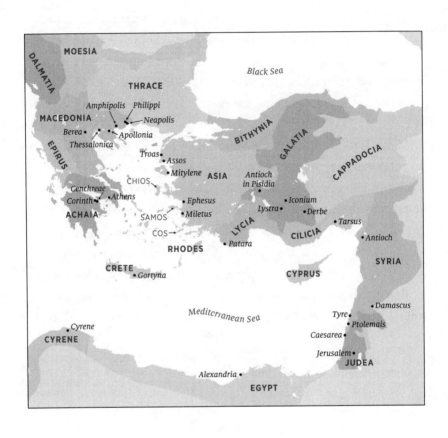

13

I Have Many in This City
Who Are My People

Acts 17:10–18:22

THE BEST WAY I KNOW to describe my friend Mary Trapnell is to say that she is bottled sunshine. With her blond hair, brilliant smile, and contagious laugh, she lights up whatever space she enters. And what I really love about her is that she takes that light to the darkest of places.

A while ago, Mary became aware that a certain motel on the edge of the city she grew up in held a cadre of women pimped by human traffickers. And she just couldn't look the other way and get on with her life of social events, school involvement, and Bible studies. What started with taking meals to the women at that motel has become an organization called Nashville Anti-Human Trafficking (NAHT),[1] which rescues women from being trafficked for sex and provides addiction recovery and other support. But what makes NAHT unique among human trafficking organizations is what drives and directs Mary and her team—the gospel of Jesus. Mary is clear that Jesus is the only hope for those being rescued, for those doing the rescuing, and for

1   You can learn more about NAHT at https://www.nahtcoalition.org.

those doing the trafficking of women and purchasing sex from them. Having been told numerous times along the way that she could raise more money and have more impact if she would just tamp down on the Jesus stuff, Mary has not backed down from keeping Jesus at the center of everything NAHT does. Why? Because when Mary looks at the city, she sees people literally trapped in sin, and she knows that only Jesus saves.

We're traveling along with Paul on his second missionary journey and seeing that, as he makes his way from city to city, he will not back down from keeping Jesus at the center of everything. Why? Because he knows there are people in that city who are trapped in sin and that only Jesus saves.

Paul's Message to the Bereans: Jesus Is the Promised Christ

After leaving Thessalonica in the middle of the night, Paul and Silas made their way to Berea, where they did what they always did whenever they came to a new city: they went to the Jewish synagogue.

> Now these Jews were more noble than those in Thessalonica; they received the word with all eagerness, examining the Scriptures daily to see if these things were so. (17:11)

Every day when the scrolls were read in the synagogue, Paul rose to speak, pointing out how the passage had been fulfilled in the person and work of Jesus of Nazareth. I imagine he was like a broken record—no matter what they read from the Old Testament he helped them to see its connection to Jesus.[2] While the Jews in Thessalonica had responded

---

2   I propose eight things to look for in an Old Testament passage to get to Christ: (1) a problem that only Christ can solve; (2) a promise that only Christ can fulfill; (3) a need that only Christ can meet; (4) a pattern or theme that only comes to resolution in Christ; (5) a story that only comes to its conclusion through Christ; (6) a person who prefigures an aspect of who Christ will be or what he will do by analogy and/or contrast; (7) an event or symbol that pictures an aspect of who Christ will be or what he will do; (8) a revelation of the preincarnate Christ.

to his message by forming a mob to attack them, the Jews in Berea were open to what Paul and Silas had to say. Rather than dismiss their message that Jesus is the Christ out of hand, the Bereans were willing to vigorously examine whether what they read in the scrolls of the Old Testament scriptures lined up with what Paul presented. And some of them were given eyes to see that Jesus truly is the promised Christ.

> Many of them therefore believed, with not a few Greek women of high standing as well as men. (17:12)

It appears that those who rejected what Paul presented did so peaceably—at least until the Jews who had run Paul and Silas out of Thessalonica showed up.

> But when the Jews from Thessalonica learned that the word of God was proclaimed by Paul at Berea also, they came there too, agitating and stirring up the crowds. Then the brothers immediately sent Paul off on his way to the sea, but Silas and Timothy remained there. Those who conducted Paul brought him as far as Athens, and after receiving a command for Silas and Timothy to come to him as soon as possible, they departed. (17:13–15)

Paul and Silas were not anxious to cause a disruption in the city of Berea, so a few of the believers took Paul and set sail with him to the great city of Athens, leaving Silas and Timothy to join him later.

Paul's Message to the Athenians: Jesus Is the Returning Judge

Arriving in Athens by himself, we get the sense that rather than heading directly to the synagogue on his own, Paul explored the city. Athens was the city of Socrates and Plato, a city of intellect and art. But Paul was not particularly impressed by the city. There was something he saw in the city that to him was like a kick in the gut.

> Now while Paul was waiting for them at Athens, his spirit was pro-
> voked within him as he saw that the city was full of idols. (17:16)

Everywhere Paul looked, he saw statues, altars, and temples built
for the worship of a plethora of Greek gods. Dominating the acropolis
was a gleaming statue of Athena, the goddess of wisdom and warfare
who took her name from the city. But she wasn't alone. There were
idols everywhere Paul looked. As he took them in, he felt sick to his
stomach. I wonder if he was struggling to hold back tears. It wasn't so
much the idols themselves that bothered him, since he knew they had
no real existence. It was the pervasive hold idolatry had over the people
of Athens that was so upsetting to Paul. Everywhere he looked, Paul
saw myriads of people deceived into thinking these made-up gods were
worthy of their worship. He saw people destined to perish estranged
from the one true God. In addition to his compassion for the lost people
of Athens, Paul felt a deep sense of jealousy for the glory of God as he
saw human beings giving the honor and glory due to the one true God
to hundreds of false gods.

Though Paul was disgusted by what he saw, he didn't write off the
city or the people. Instead, he began to engage.

> So he reasoned in the synagogue with the Jews and the devout per-
> sons, and in the marketplace every day with those who happened
> to be there. Some of the Epicurean and Stoic philosophers also
> conversed with him. (17:17–18a)

In addition to spending time in the synagogue, he was also spending time every day in the marketplace. This was not simply a marketplace of merchandise; it was a marketplace of ideas. The Epicureans
were there saying that everything is made up of atoms that randomly
swerve together. Their message: the goal of life is to pursue pleasure and avoid pain. The Stoics were there suggesting that god is in

everything. Their message: everything is determined by fate, so learn to go with the flow.

And then came Paul into the marketplace talking about the one true God and his Son, Jesus Christ, who lived and died and rose from the dead. Evidently the Athenian philosophers weren't particularly impressed with what Paul had to say.

And some said, "What does this babbler wish to say?" (17:18b)

Calling Paul a "babbler" was an insult. The word pictures a bird picking up seeds and spitting them out without digesting them. By calling Paul a "babbler" they were suggesting that Paul had picked at religious scraps from the gutters of the world to construct his argument without understanding any of it. In other words, they were suggesting that Paul wasn't very smart.

Others said, "He seems to be a preacher of foreign divinities"— because he was preaching Jesus and the resurrection. (17:18c)

They thought they had heard of all the gods. But they had never heard of this Jesus. All the religions they were used to hearing about had a kind of sameness because of their human origins. But Paul was telling them about a God who became human and rose from the dead to save sinners. It was unlike anything they had ever heard.

If this guy was putting forth a new god to be considered for their pantheon of gods, that would need to be adjudicated by the council of the Areopagus. So that's where they took Paul.

And they took him and brought him to the Areopagus, saying, "May we know what this new teaching is that you are presenting? For you bring some strange things to our ears. We wish to know therefore what these things mean." Now all the Athenians and the foreigners who lived there would spend their time in nothing except telling or hearing something new. So Paul, standing in the midst of the Areopagus, said: "Men of Athens, I perceive that in every way you are very religious. For as I passed along and observed the objects of your worship, I found also an altar with this inscription: 'To the unknown god.'" (17:19–23a)

As Paul had made his way through the city, he had come upon a particular altar that caught his attention. There was no idol with this altar since that would have required that the idol makers knew something about the characteristics and attributes of the god, and this god was not known. In a sense this was their "just in case" altar. Just in case there was a god that hadn't been acknowledged in the pantheon of gods, they had built this altar to give that god its due. Paul used this idea of a god they didn't know to present to them the one true God.

What therefore you worship as unknown, this I proclaim to you. The God who made the world and everything in it, being Lord of heaven and earth, does not live in temples made by man, nor is he served by human hands, as though he needed anything, since he himself gives to all mankind life and breath and everything. (17:23b–25)

Paul is speaking to people who have no familiarity with or regard for the Hebrew scriptures as those at the synagogue do, so he begins with what they do know and regard: the creation. By saying that God made the world and everything in it, Paul is presenting a very different view of reality from that of the Epicureans, who said that the world came to be through atoms swerving through space, and very different from the Stoics, who said that everything is god.

Surrounded by the temples to the Greek gods, Paul says that the one true God doesn't live in temples made by human hands. This God doesn't demand the kind of gifts and sacrifices their gods demand. Instead, this God gives mankind everything good, including life itself. Paul continues:

And he made from one man every nation of mankind to live on all the face of the earth, having determined allotted periods and the boundaries of their dwelling place, that they should seek God, and perhaps feel their way toward him and find him. Yet he is actually not far from each one of us. (17:26–27)

In other words, this God not only made the world; he has directed the course of history and the development of peoples and nations who have all descended from the first man, Adam. And he has done this for a particular purpose: "that they should seek God" (v. 27). Their idolatry, he says, represents their attempt to "feel their way" toward the real God, a search for something divine outside of themselves. And he has good news for them: the God who, to this point, has been unknown to them has made himself known! Indeed, Paul asserts, their own poets have displayed some sense of the one true God. And so he quotes one, saying:

"In him we live and move and have our being." (17:28a)

Using a quote from a song written about Zeus by Epimenides, a line they would have been familiar with, Paul says that greatest pursuit of life is to seek and to find the one true God. The pantheon of Greek gods was the means to other things—prosperity, victory, wisdom, fertility, beauty. Paul presents a God who is so glorious and transcendent that he is his own reward. To lay hold of him is to live.

Paul continues with a quote from a poem called "Phaenomena" written by the Stoic poet Aratus.

"As even some of your own poets have said,
  'For we are indeed his offspring.'" (17:28b)

Paul is familiar enough with their culture to be able to use their own poetry to make his point—that every person has been made in the image of the Creator. He's taking a line from familiar poetry and suggesting that their poets have stumbled onto truth.[3] And he builds on that.

> "Being then God's offspring, we ought not to think that the divine being is like gold or silver or stone, an image formed by the art and imagination of man." (17:29)

Throughout the city were idols made with gold or silver or stone.[4] Paul is saying, "How can you think that the God who made you can be reduced to something you can make with your hands out of metal or stone?"

Next, Paul transitions into the implications of the unknown god being made known to them.

> "The times of ignorance God overlooked, but now he commands all people everywhere to repent." (17:30)

Paul is saying that up to this time, God has not brought down judgment on the world for its willful ignorance of him. But that will not always be the case, especially now that he has revealed himself in his Son. Why should all people everywhere—including these Greek idol worshipers and philosophers—repent of their willful ignorance of God?

> "Because he has fixed a day on which he will judge the world in righteousness by a man whom he has appointed; and of this he has given assurance to all by raising him from the dead." (17:31)

---

3   This use of lines from their own poets reminds me of what I think is the most-often-quoted-in-sermons line of poetry from a song from our own modern culture. How many times have you heard someone quote Bob Dylan's song "Gotta Serve Somebody" to make the point that we all worship something or someone? Paul is doing something similar here.

4   The pagans would have said that the images made of metal and stone were only visual reminders of the gods, but even as reminders they were false, as they were even less than human beings. "They have mouths but do not speak; eyes, but do not see. They have ears, but do not hear; noses, but do not smell" (Ps. 115:5–6).

The return of Jesus is the next big event on the calendar of redemptive history. And when he comes again, he will come to judge. To the Epicureans, who pursued pleasure with no sense of accountability, Paul's message was: You are accountable to the one true God. To the Stoics, who dignified resignation to fate, Paul's message was: Your destiny is not determined by fate. You can repent and face the coming day of judgment without fear.

> Now when they heard of the resurrection of the dead, some mocked. But others said, "We will hear you again about this." So Paul went out from their midst. But some men joined him and believed, among whom also were Dionysius the Areopagite and a woman named Damaris and others with them. (17:32–34)

For some who gathered before the council of the Areopagus, and for at least one person on the council (Dionysius), the day began with an interest in hearing what Paul had to say in the marketplace, continued with mocking him as scavenging like a bird for bits of insight. But then they heard his message of Jesus as the coming judge and resurrected Lord, and they determined to put all of their hope in what Paul presented as being true. Some who heard him left behind their worship of idols made of metal and stone that could never save them, taking hold of the one true God who became flesh in order to save them.

Paul's Message to the Corinthians: Jesus Is the Sovereign Savior

As chapter 18 opens, Paul has left Athens and traveled 46 miles east to the city of Corinth. The capital city of Achaia (modern-day Greece), Corinth was a large city of commerce, celebrity, sexual license, and religious diversity. Overlooking the city was the temple to Aphrodite, the goddess of sexual love and beauty. Within the city was the stadium of Corinth where the Isthmian games were held during the "off" years of the Olympic Games.

And he found a Jew named Aquila, a native of Pontus, recently come from Italy with his wife Priscilla, because Claudius had commanded all the Jews to leave Rome. (18:2)

Because of the conflict between Christian and non-Christian Jews, which upset the Pax Romana, Aquila and Priscilla were two of many Jews who had been expelled from Rome by Claudius.

And he went to see them, and because he was of the same trade he stayed with them and worked, for they were tentmakers by trade. (18:3)

Aquila and Priscilla were there, settled into their tent-making trade, when Paul arrived needing a place to stay and way to earn his keep.

And he reasoned in the synagogue every Sabbath, and tried to persuade Jews and Greeks. When Silas and Timothy arrived from Macedonia, Paul was occupied with the word, testifying to the Jews that the Christ was Jesus. And when they opposed and reviled him, he shook out his garments and said to them, "Your blood be on your own heads! I am innocent. From now on I will go to the Gentiles." (18:4–6)

As was his custom, Paul went first to the synagogue where he did what he always did among those who were familiar with the Old Testament text—seek to show them that Jesus of Nazareth was the Christ promised in the Scriptures. But the Jews in Corinth were having none of it. So he left the synagogue with what can sound like harsh words: "Your blood be on your own heads!" But, in reality, Paul was simply making clear that while he was responsible to present the gospel to them, he was not responsible for their response. They would suffer the inevitable consequences of their rejection of Christ.

What is interesting (and a bit humorous) is that when Paul left the synagogue, he didn't go far.

And he left there and went to the house of a man named Titius Justus, a worshiper of God. His house was next door to the synagogue. (18:7)

We're going to read that Paul stayed in Corinth for eighteen months, and we know that the church continued long after he left. What a rub it must have been to the rejecting Jews meeting in the synagogue to have to pass the church next door, bustling with joyful new believers. And to add insult to injury, we read:

Crispus, the ruler of the synagogue, believed in the Lord, together with his entire household. And many of the Corinthians hearing Paul believed and were baptized. (18:8)

Not only did the Christians move in next door; they took the ruler of the synagogue with them along with his whole family and a bunch of other people too!

To this point Paul has been preaching the gospel to the Jews and God-fearing Gentiles in Corinth. Now it is time for him to engage with the pagans of the city. As much opposition as Paul has dealt with to this point, we might think he would be immune from fear or anxiety in regard to taking the gospel to people who've never heard it. But evidently not.

And the Lord said to Paul one night in a vision, "Do not be afraid, but go on speaking and do not be silent, for I am with you, and no one will attack you to harm you." (18:9–10)

The Lord's first words to Paul are, "Do not be afraid." Paul is not super-human. In fact, he will describe exactly how he felt in a letter he will write to the church in Corinth after he leaves the city. "I was with you in weakness and in fear and much trembling" (1 Cor. 2:3). Paul is weak and fearful, so in a vision God assured Paul of his presence and his protection. He also filled Paul with a sense of purpose.

"For I have many in this city who are my people." And he stayed a year and six months, teaching the word of God among them. (18:10–11)

Think for a moment about what you see when you drive toward a city. You see its skyline of tall buildings, its signs touting attractions. When visitors entered the city of Corinth, they would have seen the shrine to Aphrodite on the mountain, the markets, the stadium, and the ships in the ports. But what did Jesus see when he looked at the city of Corinth? Jesus saw people who didn't yet know that they were his.

We can almost hear Paul saying to people in Corinth over the months to come, "You may have always seen yourself as belonging to this city with all its vices and pleasures. But actually, before you were born, God knew you, and marked you out as his own. Won't you come to know the Jesus who has known you all along?"

Paul will also later write to the Corinthians, "For I decided to know nothing among you except Jesus Christ and him crucified" (1 Cor. 2:2). So once again, we can almost hear Paul saying to the Corinthians, "Jesus, who dwelt in the purity of heaven, came to the corrupt city of man. He came because he knew there were many in the city who belonged to him. He saw us in our idolatry and sensuality and immorality and was provoked. So he engaged, telling us the truth about our idols and their inability to provide the significance, security, and salvation we need. Though we were completely identified with this world and its ways of thinking, valuing, and living, he drew us to himself with gospel promises of a new identity of being one of God's own people. On the cross he took upon himself our arrogance and pride, our snobbery and idolatry, our lust for sex and money and power, so that when we come to him, he welcomes us with open arms, saying, 'You are my people. Welcome home.' "

You and I live in a world of sophistication that collectively rolls its eyes when we suggest that Jesus saves. It was no less so in Athens or in Corinth in Paul's day. As Paul called people who defined themselves by their lives in Corinth to instead define themselves by their belonging to Christ, he kept Jesus—the sovereign Savior and crucified Christ—at the center. He knew that only Jesus saves.

That same conviction is what keeps my friend Mary getting up every morning to engage with the unseemly side of the city. She looks at the city, and she feels its pain in her gut. But instead of condemning it, or withdrawing from it, she engages with it. God has given her eyes to see that there are many in the city who don't yet know that they belong to Jesus.

Let's ask the Spirit to give us eyes to see and hearts to love those around us who have no interest in and see no need for a God they don't know. Let's engage, believing that there are many in our city who belong to Jesus. Let's tell them that Jesus saves.

14

The Word Continued to Increase and Prevail Mightily

Acts 18:23–20:38

ARE THERE SOME BOOKS you've loaned to people and didn't get back that you kind of mourn? One of those for me would be the book *Children Are Wet Cement*, which the author, Anne Ortlund, signed and gave to me when she visited me during my maternity leave after I had my son Matt. I loved that book. Its message of how the words of parents make a deep impression on their children resonated with me deeply, causing me to think deeply about some of the words that had shaped me and making me want to use my words to make the best possible impression in the wet cement of my son's life.

In the book of Acts, we're reading about the infant church, and there is a word that is making deep impressions on the wet cement of their lives—the word of God.

The word is at work shaping and changing people and communities—in fact the entire known world. At the end of the first section of Acts that focused on the spread of the gospel in Jerusalem, we read, "The word of God continued to increase, and the number of the disciples multiplied greatly in Jerusalem" (6:7). Then, after the Holy Spirit fell on the Gentiles, and the church was established in Antioch, we again read, "The word of God increased and multiplied" (12:24). In the passage we'll consider in this chapter, the gospel comes to Ephesus, the capital city of Asia. And unsurprisingly we will read, "So the word of the Lord continued to increase and prevail mightily" (19:20).

But notice that this repeated idea is stated with a slight difference this time. It has been *increasing*, and here we read that it is *prevailing*. Prevailing over what, and in what way? What kind of word is this that is making such a deep impression on the pagan world of the Roman Empire and specifically the city of Ephesus? Let's work our way through Acts 18:23 to the end of chapter 20 to find out.[1]

An Accurate Word

We're turning our focus to the city of Ephesus, the capital city of Asia, where someone is having an impact before Paul gets there.

> Now a Jew named Apollos, a native of Alexandria, came to Ephesus. He was an eloquent man, competent in the Scriptures. He had been instructed in the way of the Lord. And being fervent in spirit, he spoke and taught accurately the things concerning Jesus, though he knew only the baptism of John. He began to speak boldly in the synagogue, but when Priscilla and Aquila heard him, they took him aside and explained to him the way of God more accurately. (18:24–26)

Greeks love their powerful orators. And evidently Apollos is one of those. He's eloquent and competent in the Scriptures. Those who heard him speak would have said, "He's on fire!" Priscilla and Aquila, who had spent eighteen months living and working with Paul in Corinth,

---

1   Because this is a large section of Scripture, this chapter will not reproduce or discuss every part of the text. If you're doing a study of Acts, you'll want to be sure to read the entirety of the text and/or complete the companion personal Bible study, which will cover the entirety of this passage.

are now in Ephesus, and when they hear Apollos speak, they hear some things that don't quite line up with Scripture and what they'd heard Paul teach. So they have a private conversation with Apollos to point out how his presentation of the gospel could more closely align with the Scriptures and apostolic teaching. What a beautiful thing, this godly couple loving God's word enough to want it to be taught rightly, and loving Apollos enough to correct him in private. And what a beautiful thing that, rather than responding with, "Why don't you stick to your tent-making and leave the teaching to me?" Apollos humbly receives and incorporates what they show him so that as he moves on from Ephesus to Achaia, he's able to more accurately show "by the Scriptures that the Christ was Jesus" (18:28). The more accurate word has prevailed over the less accurate word in the ministry of Apollos, filling his ministry with gospel power.

A Complete Word

Years earlier, Paul had been forbidden by the Holy Spirit to go to Asia, but finally he made it to Ephesus.

> There he found some disciples. And he said to them, "Did you receive the Holy Spirit when you believed?" And they said, "No, we have not even heard that there is a Holy Spirit." And he said, "Into what then were you baptized?" They said, "Into John's baptism." And Paul said, "John baptized with the baptism of repentance, telling the people to believe in the one who was to come after him, that is, Jesus." On hearing this, they were baptized in the name of the Lord Jesus. And when Paul had laid his hands on them, the Holy Spirit came on them, and they began speaking in tongues and prophesying. There were about twelve men in all. (19:1–7)

When we read that Paul found some disciples in Ephesus, it is not clear whose disciples they are. Perhaps someone who had heard John the Baptist preaching a baptism of repentance to prepare for the Christ who was to come had brought that message to these men. As Paul explains that John told people to believe in the one who was to come after him, Jesus, it seems to indicate that they hadn't heard that the Christ had come in the person of Jesus and that he had lived, died, resurrected, ascended, and then sent his Spirit to indwell believers. They had heard a bit of truth regarding God's work in the world but not the complete truth of the gospel of Jesus. But when they heard the complete word, they received it and were baptized into it. The complete word has prevailed over partial truth in the lives of these twelve men in Ephesus.

A Bold Word

As was his custom, Paul began his ministry in Ephesus at the synagogue, focusing on the Jews who gathered there. Daily he "spoke boldly, reasoning and persuading them about the kingdom of God" (19:8). Paul knew it was the word of the kingdom of God fulfilled in Jesus Christ that they needed to hear, so that's what he talked about day after day for three months.

> But when some became stubborn and continued in unbelief, speaking evil of the Way before the congregation, he withdrew from them and took the disciples with him, reasoning daily in the hall of Tyrannus. This continued for two years, so that all the residents of Asia heard the word of the Lord, both Jews and Greeks. (19:9–10)

Paul gets up every day in Ephesus and heads to the "hall of Tyrannus," a place in the city where people engage in public debate. And he just keeps talking about Jesus in Ephesus and in other cities in Asia until the word of the Lord has made its way throughout the region. This bold word is not being silenced by unbelieving Jews; it's spreading. It can't be stopped by insult or misrepresentation. And it can't be hindered by distance or by differences in ethnicity. It is prevailing over hindrances of culture and distance, impacting the whole of Asia.

A Healing Word

As Paul gives out God's word, he is doing miracles of healing that authenticate his message. His miracles catch the attention of some Jewish exorcists, who are actually sons of a Jewish high priest named Sceva, as they work their way from town to town using "magic" to make a buck.

> And God was doing extraordinary miracles by the hands of Paul, so that even handkerchiefs or aprons that had touched his skin were carried away to the sick, and their diseases left them and the evil spirits came out of them. Then some of the itinerant Jewish exorcists undertook to invoke the name of the Lord Jesus over those who had evil spirits, saying, "I adjure you by the Jesus whom Paul proclaims." (19:11–13)

Paul has been healing people in the name of Jesus, so these Jewish exorcists decide they'll try using the same words that Paul uses, hoping to appropriate the power of the name of Jesus for their purpose and to line their own pockets. But it doesn't exactly go the way they thought it would.

> But the evil spirit answered them, "Jesus I know, and Paul I recognize, but who are you?" (19:15)

Well, that's awkward! We see again and again throughout the Gospels that demons know exactly who Jesus is. They have submitted to him and to his apostolic representatives. But they don't know these guys who are seeking to use the name of Jesus.

> And the man in whom was the evil spirit leaped on them, mastered all of them and overpowered them, so that they fled out of that house

naked and wounded. And this became known to all the residents of Ephesus, both Jews and Greeks. And fear fell upon them all, and the name of the Lord Jesus was extolled. Also many of those who were now believers came, confessing and divulging their practices. And a number of those who had practiced magic arts brought their books together and burned them in the sight of all. And they counted the value of them and found it came to fifty thousand pieces of silver. (19:16–19)

Notice who is burning their magic books. It is new believers in Christ (19:18). Evidently they had not yet put away their old way of life, dabbling in magic. Then they see or hear about the seven sons of the high priest running down the street naked after trying to misappropriate the name of Jesus. Everybody in town is talking about it, recognizing the power in the name of Jesus that is different from, and superior to, any power they had seen or experienced before. So why are they still dabbling in magic? They are ready to be done with it. At that point, they don't care how much they had invested in this old way of life. They no longer want to live by their magic books; they want to live by another book, the word of God. They want an ongoing experience of its power to bring healing and wholeness to their lives.

It is following this story that we read those important summary words:

So the word of the Lord continued to increase and prevail mightily. (19:20)

The accurate word has prevailed over the clever but less accurate word. The complete word has prevailed over an incomplete understanding of the gospel. The bold word has prevailed over those who sought to silence it. And now the healing word of the name of Jesus has prevailed over those who have sought to misappropriate its power for their own purposes. The word of the Lord is prevailing mightily.

A Dangerous Word

Of course, not everyone in Ephesus was excited about the impact the word of the Lord was having throughout Asia. One guy in particular, the head of the silversmith union, was particularly bothered by the way the increasing and prevailing word of the Lord was cutting into the profits of those in the silver shrine trade.

> About that time there arose no little disturbance concerning the Way. For a man named Demetrius, a silversmith, who made silver shrines of Artemis, brought no little business to the craftsmen. These he gathered together, with the workmen in similar trades, and said, "Men, you know that from this business we have our wealth. And you see and hear that not only in Ephesus but in almost all of Asia this Paul has persuaded and turned away a great many people, saying that gods made with hands are not gods." (19:23–26)

Imagine that. Paul has the audacity to suggest that the little shrines these craftsmen are making in their workshops are not real gods! Demetrius continues:

> "And there is danger not only that this trade of ours may come into disrepute but also that the temple of the great goddess Artemis may be counted as nothing, and that she may even be deposed from her magnificence, she whom all Asia and the world worship." (19:27)

The word of God is a dangerous word. It poses a real danger to false worship and predatory religiosity. When the word of God, which is true and real, prevails over the worship of anything and everything that is not worthy of the worship that belongs to God alone, those idols end up "counted as nothing." They're deposed from their magnificence in our lives. Isn't this exactly what we want the word of God to do in our lives, even though it feels as though our pattern of living life as we please is seriously being put in danger?

> When [the workmen] heard this they were enraged and were crying out, "Great is Artemis of the Ephesians!" So the city was filled with the confusion, and they rushed together into the theater, dragging with them Gaius and Aristarchus, Macedonians who were Paul's companions in travel. (19:28–29)

None of us likes to have our idols dethroned or our financial security threatened. And we tend to want those around us to join us in the worship of our idols. We feel rage at whatever or whoever is exposing them for what they are. Demetrius has created such an uproar in the city that people are joining into the fracas without fully understanding what is going on. But then the town clerk quiets the crowd and begins to speak:

> "Men of Ephesus, who is there who does not know that the city of the Ephesians is temple keeper of the great Artemis, and of the sacred stone that fell from the sky?" (19:35)

A sacred stone that fell from the sky? Meteorites were associated with Artemis worship. So probably a meteorite fell from the sky at some point, and they saw it as coming from Zeus and so made it an object of worship in their temple to the goddess Artemis. Veneration of the sacred stone is being threatened by the word of the Lord. The word of the Lord has proved to be a dangerous word, at work to depose the magnificence of false idols in the lives of the residents of Ephesus, and in our lives as well.

That empire-wide commitment to peace, the Pax Romana, seems to kick in, and the crowd is dispersed. And when the uproar ceases, Paul says farewell to his brothers and sisters in Ephesus for the time being.

Paul resolved in the Spirit to pass through Macedonia and Achaia and go to Jerusalem, saying, "After I have been there, I must also see Rome." (19:21)

An Encouraging Word

As Paul visited the various churches he had planted throughout Macedonia, he delivered a word of encouragement.

> When he had gone through those regions and had given them much encouragement, he came to Greece. There he spent three months. (20:2–3)

I imagine the young churches in these pagan cities needed some encouragement. What is the content or method of the "much encouragement" Paul provided to them? It was the word of God. The wisdom, truth, and power of the word of God prevailed over any lurking discouragement so that they were strengthened to keep on believing in Jesus and to keep on speaking of another King, Jesus, in these cities under the rule of Caesar.

> We sailed away from Philippi after the days of Unleavened Bread, and in five days we came to them at Troas, where we stayed for seven days. (20:6)

He's there to encourage them. And clearly, as they gather to have the Lord's Supper together and hear the word preached on the Lord's Day, knowing this will be his last time to be with them, Paul has a lot to say.

> On the first day of the week, when we were gathered together to break bread, Paul talked with them, intending to depart on the next day, and he prolonged his speech until midnight. There were many

lamps in the upper room where we were gathered. And a young man named Eutychus, sitting at the window, sank into a deep sleep as Paul talked still longer. And being overcome by sleep, he fell down from the third story and was taken up dead. But Paul went down and bent over him, and taking him in his arms, said, "Do not be alarmed, for his life is in him." (20:7–10)

Any of us who have ever struggled to stay awake during a long sermon or watched someone else trying but failing to stay awake can't help but find some humor in this story. Of course, few of us have ever sat through a sermon anywhere near as long as this one. Did you catch it? Paul began speaking on the Lord's Day and then he "prolonged his speech" (20:7). Then "Paul talked still longer" (20:9). He kept talking all day until midnight when he was interrupted by the upset caused by Eutychus falling asleep and falling out of the window. We might want to hear more about Paul taking him in his arms and apparently bringing him back to life from having died from the fall, but the text seems to want us to focus on something else. We get one verse on this miracle and then we're told:

And when Paul had gone up and had broken bread and eaten, he conversed with them a long while, until daybreak, and so departed. And they took the youth away alive, and were not a little comforted. (20:11–12)

The focus is on the encouraging word Paul was sharing with them. A man was brought back to life, and Paul seemed to simply pick up where he left off to talk another six hours! It is the encouraging word, more than the miracle, that will sustain these disciples in the work of the gospel over the months and years to come. The miracle simply wasn't the most important thing that happened that night. The encouragement of believers with the word of the Lord was the important thing.

A Profitable Word

Paul headed out from Troas to make his way to Jerusalem. Luke traces Paul's journey by foot and by boat along the west coast of Asia, finally landing at Miletus, 36 miles south of Ephesus (20:13–14). From Miletus, he sent word to the elders of the church in Ephesus to come to him for what would be a profitable word, in some ways a painful word, and significantly his final word to them in person.

> And when they came to him, he said to them: "You yourselves know how I lived among you the whole time from the first day that I set foot in Asia, serving the Lord with all humility and with tears and with trials that happened to me through the plots of the Jews; how I did not shrink from declaring to you anything that was profitable, and teaching you in public and from house to house, testifying both to Jews and to Greeks of repentance toward God and of faith in our Lord Jesus Christ." (20:18–21)

When Paul summarized what he'd said to the Ephesian church over the two years and three months he had spent with them, he said he had focused on what would be profitable to them, what would add to their lives, what would prove beneficial to them in the fight of faith. He'd spoken the word of God to them in the formal setting of the church meeting. And he'd gone house to house. Evidently, whenever he'd come over for dinner, one thing dominated the conversation—the word of Christ—which proved profitable to them in their lives of faith.

> And now, behold, I am going to Jerusalem, constrained by the Spirit, not knowing what will happen to me there, except that the Holy Spirit testifies to me in every city that imprisonment and afflictions await me. But I do not account my life of any value nor as precious to myself, if only I may finish my course and the ministry that

I received from the Lord Jesus, to testify to the gospel of the grace
of God. (20:22–24)

As he sets his sights on Jerusalem, Paul expects the word of God
to go on prevailing wherever he speaks it, but he doesn't expect that
to come without personal cost. In fact, the Holy Spirit has told him
what he can expect. He can expect to be put in jail. He can expect to
be mistreated. When Paul looks into the future, it is saturated with
suffering. But he's not focused on or deterred by that; he's determined
in that. He's determined to keep on testifying to the gospel of the grace
of God. This is the word that prevails: the word of grace for sinners.
It's such good news. He's not about to stop giving it out.

And now, behold, I know that none of you among whom I have
gone about proclaiming the kingdom will see my face again. (20:25)

This must have been hard for those Ephesian elders to hear. They
loved him. They had been "separated from Christ, alienated from the
commonwealth of Israel and strangers to the covenants of promise,
having no hope and without God in the world." And then Paul came
and spoke the word of God to them, and it prevailed over their sepa-
ration and alienation so that now these Ephesians who "once were far
off have been brought near by the blood of Christ" (Eph. 2:12–13).
He will write to them, but he would not see them again in this life.

Therefore I testify to you this day that I am innocent of the blood
of all, for I did not shrink from declaring to you the whole counsel
of God. (20:26–27)

Paul leaves with a clear conscience. If there are those in Ephesus who
perish in unbelief, it won't be because Paul squandered the opportunity
to present the gospel of the grace of Jesus to them when he was given the

opportunity. He knew that what he presented to them was not merely a little inspiration for the day, a little good advice, or pop religiosity for profit. He gave them the full load of truth, everything they needed for salvation, "the whole counsel of God."

Before he leaves, Paul warns the elders that threats are going to arise within the church from some who will purport to have a word from God, but really what they have to say will be off. It will be less than "the whole counsel of God." So they must keep rehearsing this word they've heard from Paul, a word marked by one thing in particular: grace.

> And now I commend you to God and to the word of his grace, which is able to build you up and to give you the inheritance among all those who are sanctified. (20:32)

The word of grace! This is the word that prevails! The word of God isn't simply a story, though it is a story. It isn't simply a set of rules, though it contains a revelation of God's character and will for those who belong to him. It is a word of the grace made available to sinners through the life, death, and resurrection of Jesus, a word that has the power not only to save but also to sanctify. This word of the grace of Jesus has the power to keep the church in Ephesus strong and growing in godliness.

> And when he had said these things, he knelt down and prayed with them all. And there was much weeping on the part of all; they embraced Paul and kissed him, being sorrowful most of all because of the word he had spoken, that they would not see his face again. And they accompanied him to the ship. (20:36–38)

Over the course of more than two years, the word that Paul had spoken to them—the whole counsel of God, the word of grace—had made deep impressions in the wet cement of their lives. It had prevailed over confusion, over sickness, over error, ignorance, alienation, and evil. As they looked toward the future, they prayed it would prevail over discouragement and opposition.

Indeed, this is the word we need to make a deep and lasting impression in the wet cement of our own lives. We need this word of grace to tell us the full truth, convict us of sin, correct our misunderstandings, clarify our confusion, heal our brokenness, build us up, encourage us, purify us. We need this word of grace to get the final, defining, saving word in our lives.

MOESIA

DALMATIA

THRACE

Amphipolis *Philippi*

MACEDONIA
Berea • •Neapolis
Thessalonica •Apollonia

EPIRUS

Troas•
•*Assos*

•*Mitylene* ASIA
CHIOS

Cenchreae
Corinth• •*Athens*

ACHAIA
SAMOS •*Ephesus*
•*Miletus*

COS→

RHODES

CRETE
•*Gortyna*

Cyrene

CYRENE

BITHYNIA

GALATIA

CAPPADOCIA

Antioch
in Pisidia
•

LYCIA
Lystra• •*Iconium*
•*Derbe*

•*Tarsus*
CILICIA
•*Antioch*

SYRIA

•*Patara*

CYPRUS

Black Sea

Mediterranean Sea

•*Damascus*
Tyre•
•*Ptolemais*
Caesarea•

Jerusalem•
JUDEA

Alexandria •

EGYPT

15

Paul Resolved in His Spirit
to Go to Jerusalem

Acts 21:1–23:35

WHEN THEY WERE NEWLY MARRIED, my friends Dave and Robin Dillard were involved in a church that began to pray for unreached people groups. They somewhat randomly, or so they thought, picked the Kurds, who live in contiguous areas of Iran, Iraq, and Turkey. Their small group began to pray for the gospel to go to the Kurdish people. And then came the Gulf War along with something unexpected. Kurdish refugees began to flood into Nashville. So began a team that started Servant Group International that, over the years, has built schools in and sent teachers to Iraq, continues to partner with refugee relief in Iraq, Greece, and Turkey, and offers support for refugees and migrants who settle in the Nashville area.[1]

I love what Servant Group is and what they do. And I really love their motto: "Iraq is dangerous. Go anyway."

Don't you love that? Or maybe you don't like that at all. Maybe that makes you nervous. Or maybe you think, "That's great for

---

1 You can find out more about Servant Group International at https://servantgroup.org.

somebody else, but not me." Or, "That's fine for somebody else's kids, but not mine."

We love safety. Prayers for safety are often on our lips and dominate our prayer lists. And there's nothing wrong with a desire to be safe. But I sometimes wonder if personal safety has become an accepted idol in our day, if it is more important to us than advancing the gospel of Jesus Christ in a world in which our safety cannot be guaranteed.

In chapters 21–23 of Acts, Paul is headed to Jerusalem, where his personal safety is not only not guaranteed; it is significantly in doubt. We read back in Acts 19:21 that as Paul's time in Ephesus came to a close, he "resolved in the Spirit to pass through Macedonia and Achaia and go to Jerusalem, saying, 'After I have been there, I must also see Rome.'" Then at the end of chapter 20, Paul got on a ship headed for Jerusalem. If we consult a map, we know that Jerusalem is not exactly on the way to Rome from Macedonia. It's in the opposite direction. If Paul put Rome into his GPS, it would have been telling him, all the way from Macedonia to Jerusalem, "At the next left, make a U-turn."

So why is Paul so resolute to go to Jerusalem? Paul has been on a mission to take the gospel to the Gentiles. And he has done that. But he doesn't want there to be a Gentile church and a Jewish church. He really believes, "There is neither Jew nor Greek, there is neither slave nor free, there is no male and female, for you are all one in Christ Jesus" (Gal. 3:28). He is in pursuit of unity among God's people, to grow the relationship of acceptance and fellowship between Jewish and Gentile brothers and sisters in Christ. He's taking money collected by the churches throughout Asia Minor, Asia, and Macedonia to the church in Jerusalem (Rom. 15:25–27; 1 Cor. 16:2–4; 2 Cor. 8:1–8). These new Gentile believers have never met the believers in Jerusalem, but they know that they are brothers and sisters who have a need because of famine in Judea. Paul wants the Jews in Jerusalem to feel the same way about the Gentile Christians living for Jesus throughout Asia Minor, Asia, and Macedonia.

But this trip, which is all about developing unity, will not be all sunshine and roses. It's going to involve a great deal of suffering for Paul. In fact, as we read through Luke's account of Paul's time in Jerusalem in these chapters, it seems that Luke has written it in a way that will remind us of Jesus's trip to Jerusalem, which Luke carefully traced in his Gospel. Luke 9:51 reads that Jesus set his face to go to Jerusalem. He told his disciples, "The Son of Man must suffer many things and be rejected by the elders and chief priests and scribes, and be killed, and on the third day be raised." Then, in the same breath, he impressed upon his disciples what this would mean for them: "If anyone would come after me, let him deny himself and take up his cross daily and follow me. For whoever would save his life will lose it, but whoever loses his life for my sake will save it" (Luke 9:22–24).

Here in Acts we read that Paul, like Jesus, has "set his face to go to Jerusalem." And like Jesus, he also knows that suffering awaits him there. Clearly his personal safety is not his highest priority. Paul has denied himself and taken up his cross daily to follow Christ. He's willing to lose his life for the sake of presenting to Jesus a diverse and yet unified bride made up of Jews and Gentiles (2 Cor. 11:2).

Like Jesus, Paul Set His Face to Go to Jerusalem in Spite of Certain Suffering

Acts 21 begins by reporting the route Paul took to Jerusalem. All along the way his brothers and sisters in Christ are telling him not to go because of the suffering that will certainly await him there.[2] When he

2   Interpreters differ on how to understand the disciples in Tyre telling Paul "through the Spirit" not to go on to Jerusalem. It may be an example of a mistake in the prophecy itself or in the interpretation of it. Or it may be an indication that "the Holy Spirit, who had been constraining Paul to go to Jerusalem and face the sufferings he warned him of for the sake of the Lord's name, finally left it to Paul's free choice: he did not have to go if he did not want to. . . . It is the measure of Paul's devotion to Christ that he did not think it was necessarily a prohibition to go to Jerusalem." David Gooding, *True to the Faith: The Acts of the Apostles: Defining and Defending the Gospel* (Coleraine, UK: Myrtlesfield House, 2013), 431.

gets to the house of Philip in Caesarea, he's met by a prophet named
Agabus, who has come from Jerusalem with a message.

> And coming to us, he took Paul's belt and bound his own feet and
> hands and said, "Thus says the Holy Spirit, 'This is how the Jews at
> Jerusalem will bind the man who owns this belt and deliver him into
> the hands of the Gentiles.'" When we heard this, we and the people
> there urged him not to go up to Jerusalem. (21:11–12)

Just as Jesus submitted to being bound in his mission to die for the
salvation of Jews and Gentiles, so Paul was willing to be bound to suffer in pursuit of unity among Jewish and Gentile believers. And just as
those closest to Jesus could not bear him saying that he was going to
suffer and die in Jerusalem (Mark 8:31–33), so those who were closest
to Paul (including Luke apparently, since verse 12 says "we") did not
want Paul to go forward into Jerusalem, knowing the suffering that
awaited him there.

But Paul went anyway. When Paul arrived in Jerusalem he was received gladly by his brothers and sisters in the church.

> After greeting them, he related one by one the things that God had
> done among the Gentiles through his ministry. And when they heard
> it, they glorified God. (21:19–20)

They're happy about the Gentiles coming to Christ. But there's a problem.

> And they said to him, "You see, brother, how many thousands there
> are among the Jews of those who have believed. They are all zealous
> for the law, and they have been told about you that you teach all
> the Jews who are among the Gentiles to forsake Moses, telling them
> not to circumcise their children or walk according to our customs."
> (21:20–21)

What's the problem? There are thousands of Jewish Christians in the city of Jerusalem who have not yet let go of adherence to the Mosaic law. They're still circumcising their sons and following the Jewish calendar and food laws. Word on the street is that as Paul has been teaching at the synagogues in Gentile cities, he's been encouraging the Jewish Christians living in those cities to let go of their Jewishness.

Like Jesus, Paul Was Accused of Opposing the
Mosaic Law While Submitting to Mosaic Law

Paul's message in the synagogues in every city was that the Old Testament was filled with shadows pointing to Christ and that the substance had come in the person of Jesus, making the shadows obsolete. This meant that Jews were no longer bound to strictly adhere to laws about circumcision or food or sacrifices at the temple. Jesus's fulfillment of these things made adherence to them a matter of freedom. They could if they wanted to, but they didn't have to.

There were many Jewish Christians in Jerusalem who still felt conscience-bound to circumcise their children—not in order to gain or to retain salvation, but because it had been the right thing to do their whole lives. Though Paul taught clearly that physical circumcision was an Old Testament shadow of the purity that now came through being joined to Christ, Paul had no problem with Jewish believers continuing the practice if their conscience demanded it of them, as long as they understood and agreed that physical circumcision did not produce, contribute to, or maintain their salvation. As he would have already written to the believers in Rome by this point, "a Jew is one inwardly, and circumcision is a matter of the heart, by the Spirit, not by the letter" (Rom. 2:29). Paul recognized, however, that the Jewish conscience had been shaped over many centuries to insist on the strictest observance of the Mosaic rituals. Certainly he hoped that over time these Christians would develop the habit of thinking through Old Testament ceremonial law in light of its fulfillment by Christ and lose their sense of obligation. But he did not demand that these practices be abandoned overnight. The day was quickly coming when the temple would be destroyed, which would force not only Christian Jews, but all Jews, to leave the temple way of life behind.

James was leader of the church in Jerusalem, and he wanted Paul to do something that would demonstrate to the Jewish Christians in Jerusalem that he did not disdain the Jewish way of life or deny Jewish Christians their freedom to continue observing aspects of the Old Testament ceremonial law. He encouraged Paul to accompany some men who were going to the temple to enter into a Nazarite vow and to personally pay the cost of their temple offering.

> Thus all will know that there is nothing in what they have been told about you, but that you yourself also live in observance of the law. (21:24)

And Paul agreed.

> Then Paul took the men, and the next day he purified himself along with them and went into the temple, giving notice when the days of purification would be fulfilled and the offering presented for each one of them. (21:26)

Just as Jesus lived as a Jew under its laws, being circumcised, baptized, and making treks to the temple, even though he knew he was the fulfillment of all these things, so Paul lived as a Jew among Jews, embracing its ceremony and customs, even though he knew that Jesus had fulfilled it all.

Like Jesus, Paul Was Accused of Opposing the Temple at the Temple

Evidently, also at the temple that day were some Jews from Asia who had heard Paul present Christ in their synagogues and had rejected his message. They were incensed to see Paul at the temple.

The Jews from Asia, seeing him in the temple, stirred up the whole crowd and laid hands on him, crying out, "Men of Israel, help! This is the man who is teaching everyone everywhere against the people and the law and this place. Moreover, he even brought Greeks into the temple and has defiled this holy place." (21:27–28)

Of course, Paul was not "against the people." He was a Jew of Jews. Of course, he was not teaching against the law of God. He loved God's holy law. Of course, he was not teaching against the temple. The temple was the shadow that had shown the people of God what Jesus would do in offering himself as a once-for-all sacrifice, and what he would be as the way God's people have access to God. And he had not brought Greeks into the temple. He respected its laws. Evidently, the Asian Jews had seen an Ephesian Christian with Paul in the city and simply assumed that Paul brought him into the temple (21:29).

Then all the city was stirred up, and the people ran together. They seized Paul and dragged him out of the temple, and at once the gates were shut. And as they were seeking to kill him, word came to the tribune of the cohort that all Jerusalem was in confusion. (21:30–31)

Remember how much the Romans value peace and order. And here is a huge disturbance of the peace. So the tribune, a commander of a cohort of up to one thousand Roman soldiers, arrested Paul and bound him in chains as the mob cried out, "Away with him." Paul asked the tribune if he could speak to the mob, and the tribune gave him permission.[3] Paul began by seeking to create some common ground with those enraged against him.

3   The significance of Paul speaking in Greek to the Roman authority and Aramaic to the Jewish crowd is connected to the tribune's assumption that Paul was an Egyptian who had led a band of people out to the Mount of Olives promising them that God would tear down the walls of Jerusalem so that they could overpower the Romans. The fact that Paul spoke Greek and then Aramaic convinced him otherwise.

"I am a Jew, born in Tarsus in Cilicia, but brought up in this city, educated at the feet of Gamaliel according to the strict manner of the law of our fathers, being zealous for God as all of you are this day." (22:3)

Paul completely gets their rage toward him. He'd been there, seeking to kill Jewish Christians out of a belief that he was defending God's honor. But he had been wrong about that, wrong about the believers he sought to put in chains, and, most significantly, wrong about Jesus. That became clear to him when Jesus spoke to him out of a great light from heaven. Paul tells them how "the God of our fathers" appointed him to know his will, to see and hear the Righteous One and to be a witness for him (22:14). It was at that point that Paul uttered the words that evidently were the final straw, a part of Paul's story that was simply intolerable to them.

"And [Jesus] said to me, 'Go, for I will send you far away to the Gentiles.'" (22:21)

They had listened as he recalled his approval of Stephen's stoning and his pursuit of Christians and even his experience of seeing the risen Jesus. But then he got to the issue that really angered them—his mission to the Gentiles. Paul will later write to the Ephesians that Jesus, in his death, broke down the "dividing wall of hostility" between Jews and Gentiles, that he might "reconcile us both to God in one body through the cross" (Eph. 2:14–16). This Jewish mob has no interest in breaking down the wall of hostility. And at this moment, Paul is the target of that hostility.

Up to this word they listened to him. Then they raised their voices and said, "Away with such a fellow from the earth! For he should not be allowed to live." (22:22)

The Roman tribune, Claudius Lysias, brought Paul inside to be flogged, thinking that the sting of a whip on Paul's back would help him to get to the truth of why the mob was so enraged. But before the whipping could commence, Paul said to centurion standing by, "Is it lawful for you to flog a man who is a Roman citizen and uncondemned?" (22:25). This gets the attention of Lysias and puts him in a panic, as Paul has already been bound, which should not have happened to a Roman citizen without proper cause. So the flogging is called off.

But the tribune still wants to know the real reason that the mob has said Paul shouldn't be allowed to live. So he summoned the chief priests and religious council to meet, set Paul in front of them, and stuck around to hear what would transpire.

At this point, Paul did the kind of thing someone in a caper comedy movie might do. He realizes that there are both Sadducees and Pharisees in the room and that they have significant differences with each other. The Pharisees were all about strict law-keeping and believed that the Old Testament teaches a future resurrection of the dead. The Sadducees were basically secular Jews who controlled the priesthood and enjoyed political power granted by Rome. They had jettisoned many orthodox beliefs, including belief in a resurrection of the dead. So what does Paul begin to speak about? The topic that will get them arguing with each other instead of arguing with him: resurrection.

> Now when Paul perceived that one part were Sadducees and the other Pharisees, he cried out in the council, "Brothers, I am a Pharisee, a son of Pharisees. It is with respect to the hope and the resurrection of the dead that I am on trial." And when he had said this, a dissension arose between the Pharisees and the Sadducees, and the assembly was divided. . . . Then a great clamor arose, and some of the scribes of the Pharisees' party stood up and contended sharply, "We find nothing wrong in this man. What if a spirit or an angel spoke to him?" And when the dissension became violent, the tribune, afraid

that Paul would be torn to pieces by them, commanded the soldiers to go down and take him away from among them by force and bring him into the barracks. (23:6–10)

The tribune had already come close to beating a Roman citizen, an offense for which he would certainly have been punished. He's not about to let this Roman citizen be killed under his watch, so he acts to protect Paul when the meeting turns into a melee. But it is not merely the Roman tribune who is looking after Paul.

The following night the Lord stood by him and said, "Take courage, for as you have testified to the facts about me in Jerusalem, so you must testify also in Rome." (23:11)

Surely Paul felt alone in the Roman barracks. But he wasn't alone. Jesus stood by him. Jesus, the one who knows what it's like to be the target of a Jewish mob and to be set before a corrupt Jewish council and be taken into Roman custody, is not far off. He's standing by Paul, allowing Paul to feel his presence and hear his voice, a voice encouraging him to press on and to trust that his mission to take the gospel all the way to Rome will not be cut short by a Jewish mob or a Roman court.

But that doesn't mean the Jewish mob won't give it a try.

Like Jesus, Paul Was Conspired Against by a Jewish Mob Intent on Killing Him

When it was day, the Jews made a plot and bound themselves by an oath neither to eat nor drink till they had killed Paul. There were more than forty who made this conspiracy. (23:12–13)

This is not going to turn out well for these forty men. Since we know that Paul is going to make it out of Jerusalem alive, they must either die from starvation or break their oath!

They went to the chief priests and elders and said, "We have strictly bound ourselves by an oath to taste no food till we have killed Paul. Now therefore you, along with the council, give notice to the tribune to bring him down to you, as though you were going to determine his case more exactly. And we are ready to kill him before he comes near." (23:14–15)

There's such irony here. Their charge against Paul was that he spoke against their law. But they're intent on murdering Paul, a clear violation of "You shall not murder," which was inscribed on the stone tablets of God's law (Ex. 20:13). And they seem to have the support and blessing of at least some of the chief priests and elders.

Now the son of Paul's sister heard of their ambush, so he went and entered the barracks and told Paul. (23:16)

We don't know how Paul's nephew heard about the plot to kill Paul, but certainly we can see God's hand at work to protect him. The nephew informed Paul, and Paul informed Lysias about the plot, who went to no little effort to get Paul safely out of the city.[4] As you read, try to calculate the personnel cost of his protection.

Then he called two of the centurions and said, "Get ready two hundred soldiers, with seventy horsemen and two hundred spearmen to go as far as Caesarea at the third hour of the night. Also provide mounts for Paul to ride and bring him safely to Felix the governor." (23:23–24)

He will be brought safely to Felix, but he is not safe. There is still more suffering ahead for Paul. Caesarea is going to be his home for the

---

4   Can you see that I'm starting to write like Luke now? See Acts 12:18; 14:28; 15:2; 19:23, 24; 27:20.

next two years. Just as Jesus was found innocent by Pilate, the Roman governor, yet handed over to be crucified (Luke 23:1–7), so Paul will be found innocent by Felix, the Roman governor, yet held for two years.

Paul knew that going to Jerusalem was dangerous. And he went anyway. He knew that speaking boldly to the Jewish religious leaders about his call to take the gospel to the Gentiles would not be well received. But he said it anyway. Paul refused to make an idol of personal safety. His life was not about self-preservation; it was about being on mission. And though he was bound by chains, he was free. Though he was alone in a cell, he knew that he was never alone.

The instinct to self-preservation and danger avoidance in us is strong, isn't it? Why would we think we would be willing to risk going to dangerous places when we're unwilling to go across the street or across town? We have an incredible impulse toward self-preservation and very little inclination toward self-denial. It makes us wonder if it is really possible that we could deny ourselves, take up our cross, and follow Jesus. Where do we find the resources for that?

We have the example of Paul, who, when those around him begged him to avoid the danger of going to Jerusalem, said simply, "Let the will of the Lord be done" (21:14). But more than that, we have the Spirit of Jesus living inside us. We've been baptized into the Spirit of the one who prayed, as he faced the cross, "My Father, if it be possible, let this cup pass from me; nevertheless, not as I will, but as you will" (Matt. 26:39). Oh, that we would be empowered by the Spirit to pray the same way and want the same thing! Let's pray that the Spirit of Jesus in us will overcome our instinct toward self-preservation and increase our willingness to follow Jesus wherever he leads. Following Jesus wherever he leads may be dangerous. Let's go anyway.

Sea of
Galilee

• Caesarea

Mediterranean Sea

SAMARIA

• Antipatris

Jordan
River

◇ Jerusalem

JUDEA

Dead
Sea

TO ETHIOPIA

16

I Always Take Pains to Have a Clear Conscience toward God and Man

Acts 24:1–26:32

"MY CONSCIENCE IS CLEAR." Have you ever said or thought that? It is a way of saying that you have done what you believe is right or not done what you believe would be wrong. You're not carrying around any nagging guilt.

You may have said that a time or two, but could you say that having a clear conscience is something you highly value, something that consistently motivates you?

To be honest, I'm not sure I think much about my conscience. Or maybe I do, but I don't think about it in those terms. I do know that I haven't yet returned the potholder and spatula that my neighbor brought over with some brownies long ago and that I do feel a bit guilty every time I open the drawer and see it. I suppose that's my conscience barking at me, isn't it?

It seems that one thing that drives Paul in the way he goes about his mission is to have a clear conscience. He speaks numerous times in Acts about his conscience. Paul has gotten me thinking: How might I live differently if I were to value, and evaluate, whether or not I have a clear conscience before God and man? And, perhaps more significantly, is it really possible to be self-aware about our pervasive sinfulness, especially at the level of inner thoughts and motives, and yet have a clear conscience? What do we do with a conscience that is not clear?

When we left off the story of Acts, Paul had arrived in Caesarea to stand before the Roman governor of the region, Felix, to face charges brought against him by the Jewish religious leaders. In chapter 24 we will witness Paul's trial before Felix. In chapter 25 he has another trial before Felix's successor, Festus. And in chapter 26 Paul rehearses the charges against him and his defense before King Agrippa. We'll work our way through these chapters asking and answering three questions: (1) Why is Paul on trial? (2) What is Paul's defense? (3) What is the verdict?

Why Is Paul on Trial?

Paul has been under guard at the governor's palace in Caesarea for five days when those who have accused him get to town.

> The high priest Ananias came down with some elders and a spokesman, one Tertullus. They laid before the governor their case against Paul. (24:1)

Evidently, if we go by his name, Tertullus, which is Greek, the religious leaders in Jerusalem have hired a Gentile lawyer to represent them in this Gentile court. Tertullus seems to be laying it on thick as he begins to make his case before Felix.

> "Since through you we enjoy much peace, and since by your foresight, most excellent Felix, reforms are being made for this nation, in every way and everywhere we accept this with all gratitude. But, to detain you no further, I beg you in your kindness to hear us briefly." (24:2–4)

Then Tertullus begins outlining the charges the Jewish religious leaders have made against Paul:

"For we have found this man a plague, one who stirs up riots among all the Jews throughout the world and is a ringleader of the sect of the Nazarenes. He even tried to profane the temple, but we seized him." (24:5–6)

Tertullus puts forward three basic charges:

1. Paul has stirred up riots among the Jews wherever he has gone in the world.
2. Paul is the ringleader of a sect (insinuating a heretical sect) of Judaism.
3. Paul tried to profane the temple (by bringing a Gentile into it, according to 21:28).

All of the Jewish leaders are behind Tertullus nodding their heads in affirmation. And then Felix calls on Paul to speak.

What Is Paul's Defense?

In regard to the first charge of stirring up riots, Paul says:

"You can verify that it is not more than twelve days since I went up to worship in Jerusalem, and they did not find me disputing with anyone or stirring up a crowd, either in the temple or in the synagogues or in the city." (24:11–12)

Paul has never sought to cause trouble—in Jerusalem or in any of the synagogues he has visited throughout the Gentile world. But he has often been the victim of Jewish mobs intent on beating or even killing him.

In regard to the second charge of being the ringleader of a sect, Paul admits that, yes, he belongs to those who follow the Way, which the Jewish leaders have labeled a sect.

> "But this I confess to you, that according to the Way, which they call a sect, I worship the God of our fathers, believing everything laid down by the Law and written in the Prophets, having a hope in God, which these men themselves accept, that there will be a resurrection of both the just and the unjust." (24:14–15)

According to Paul, the followers of the Way worship the same God and believe the same Scriptures that those who are accusing him do, so they can't claim that he has started his own religion. Not only that, but those who follow the Way also share the same hope that those who are accusing them do. They look expectantly for God to bring about the same thing the Pharisees say they look forward to—the resurrection of the dead.

As we've seen throughout Acts, when the apostles speak about "the resurrection of the dead," the phrase encompasses a host of realities wrapped up with the coming of the Messiah, including bodily resurrection, the end of evil, the establishment of the new creation. What no one expected was that there would be a first coming of Messiah, when these realities would be inaugurated, and then a second coming, when they would be brought into full fruition. But Paul knows that the last days have been inaugurated in the resurrection of Jesus and that the next big event on the calendar of redemptive history will be the return of Jesus as judge. When that day comes, all will stand before the judgment seat of Christ (2 Cor. 5:10). Paul says that he lives in such a way as to be prepared for judgment day.

> "So I always take pains to have a clear conscience toward both God and man." (24:16)

Paul believes that the God he serves established the governing authorities (Rom. 13:1–2, 4–5). Therefore, to rebel against them is to rebel against God. Unless the law was contrary to the law of God, he saw it as a sin to break it. Paul is saying here that his conscience is clear in regard to obeying Rome's laws about peace and order. He has not broken the law of Rome. Paul contends that the gospel both supports the rule of Caesar (Acts 25:8–12) and fulfills the hope of Israel (26:6–7). He is both a loyal citizen of Rome and a loyal son of Israel. His conscience toward God and man—human authority placed over him by God—is clear.

In the years previous, as Paul worked his way through Asia Minor and Macedonia, he was arrested numerous times, but not because he flouted local laws or authority. He showed respect for authority and was often arrested on false charges or based on false testimony. This is not to say that there was never a time the apostles disobeyed human authority. When the authorities demanded something that clearly went against what God had commanded, Peter and Paul and the other disciples determined that they had to disobey. For example, after being told by the religious council to stay quiet, Peter and John were told by an angel of the Lord, "Go and stand in the temple and speak to the people" (5:20), and they did, saying, "We must obey God rather than men" (5:29).

Paul's conscience is clear because he has not stirred up riots. Others have stirred up mobs against him. He knows that he has not been an agitator. His conscience is clear.

In regard to the third charge of profaning the temple, Paul describes exactly what happened a few days before in Jerusalem.

"Now after several years I came to bring alms to my nation and to present offerings. While I was doing this, they found me purified in the temple, without any crowd or tumult." (24:17–18)

The fact was that Paul had come to Jerusalem with a gift for the Jews who had been facing a famine. He had gone to the temple to

present offerings and was in a state of ceremonial purity. He had
not brought a Gentile into the temple; he was there with several
Jewish men who had made a Nazarite vow. He had done nothing to
profane the temple and nothing to create a disruption of the peace
at the temple.

So Paul easily refuted the three charges against him. But then he said
something else. He presented the real reason he was on trial.

> "It is with respect to the resurrection of the dead that I am on trial
> before you this day." (24:21)

All of the Pharisees believed in the resurrection of the dead. So what's
their problem with Paul and the other followers of the Way? It's that
pesky but persistent belief they have, that the resurrection of the dead
has already begun with the resurrection of Jesus as the first of all who
will one day be raised. The Pharisees don't believe that Jesus was raised
from the dead, and they certainly don't think being connected to Jesus
is required to have the hope of one day being raised yourself.

Evidently Felix is familiar enough with both Jewish and Christian
beliefs to recognize that Paul has a point. It is religious differences that
have brought about this conflict. He knows that religious differences
are of no concern to Rome. But he also wants to curry favor with the
Jewish religious leaders who have a lot of sway over the territory under
his jurisdiction. His strategy is to delay. He'll delay at least until Lysias,
the Roman tribune who sent Paul to him, can make the trip to Caesarea
to put in his two cents. Meanwhile, Felix and his wife, Drusilla, who
was Jewish, had Paul around to the house for some conversation about
Jesus. Notice the three topics of conversation:

> And as [Paul] reasoned about righteousness and self-control and the
> coming judgment, Felix was alarmed and said, "Go away for the
> present. When I get an opportunity, I will summon you." (24:25)

What might Paul have said to these two about "righteousness and self-control and the coming judgment"? Perhaps Paul drew from the letter he had already written to the church in Rome by this point, telling Felix that there was not one person who is righteous but there is a righteousness available through faith in Jesus Christ for all who believe. Perhaps Felix didn't like being told he had no hope of being righteous on his own. Felix had a history of notorious cruelty and had seduced Drusilla, who promptly divorced her husband to marry him, so perhaps the topic of self-control was not particularly appealing to them either. And perhaps his talk about a coming day when they would stand before God and give account for their lives was not something Felix and Drusilla wanted to think about. They just wanted Paul to go away.

Felix knows that Paul is innocent, but he is unwilling to declare him so in an official verdict. He's also unwilling to release him without a bribe (24:26). And evidently Lysias, the Roman tribune, never showed up. So Paul sat in custody in Caesarea for two years, and then Felix left office and was replaced by Festus.

When chapter 25 opens, it's been two years since the Jewish religious leaders charged Paul with crimes against the Jews, their customs, and the temple. It's been two years since they made the trek to Caesarea with their fancy lawyer, Tertullus, to repeat their charges in front of Felix. But evidently two years hasn't cooled their determination to see Paul pay with his life for his supposed crimes. In fact, they're not really depending on the Roman justice system to put Paul to death. They press the new governor, Festus, to bring Paul back to Jerusalem, and their plan is to ambush him along the way and kill him themselves (25:3). But Festus is unwilling to bring Paul to Jerusalem. Instead, the Jewish leaders have to make the trip, once again, to Caesarea.

Luke doesn't provide detail of the charges they made in this second Roman trial before Festus, but we can assume they made the same charges as before. Yet by Paul's response to the charges, we get the sense that perhaps they added a charge this time around that might make

Festus more likely to issue a guilty verdict against Paul. The text doesn't articulate this additional charge, but we deduce what it was based on Paul's defense against their charges:

> Paul argued in his defense, "Neither against the law of the Jews, nor against the temple, nor against Caesar have I committed any offense." (25:8)

Evidently they've charged him with something akin to treason against Caesar, perhaps using his allegiance to another king, King Jesus, as a way of charging him with something that might stick in a Roman court. They don't have a way to prove their charge of stirring up a riot, and the rest of their charges are matters of Jewish religious law rather than Roman law.

Because Festus sees the issue as a religious conflict, and because he too wants to curry favor with the Jews, Festus seems inclined to agree when the Jews demand to take Paul back to Jerusalem to be tried there. But Paul knows that in Jerusalem Festus will be under considerable pressure to side with the Jews bent on killing him. Besides, if they're accusing him of treason against Caesar, then that is a charge that should be considered in a Roman court in front of Caesar himself.

> But Paul said, "I am standing before Caesar's tribunal, where I ought to be tried. To the Jews I have done no wrong, as you yourself know very well. If then I am a wrongdoer and have committed anything for which I deserve to die, I do not seek to escape death. But if there is nothing to their charges against me, no one can give me up to them. I appeal to Caesar." Then Festus, when he had conferred with his council, answered, "To Caesar you have appealed; to Caesar you shall go." (25:10–12)

Paul's appeal to Caesar puts Festus in a bit of a pickle. As a Roman citizen, Paul has every right to appeal to Caesar. But Festus can't send

Paul to stand in front of Caesar without a substantive provable charge of a crime against Caesar. And he knows he just doesn't have that.

About this time, Herod Agrippa, who ruled over the temple in Jerusalem and several minor, primarily Gentile territories adjacent to the territory Festus oversaw for Rome, came to Caesarea. Festus saw his visit as an opportunity to take advantage of Agrippa's greater understanding of the religious and political landscape underneath this prickly case. Festus couldn't find anything Paul had done to deserve death (25:25), but maybe if the case was laid out before Agrippa and his wife, Bernice, he would find something to charge Paul with that would stick in Caesar's court.

So Festus set up a hearing for Agrippa to hear Paul's version of the charges and his defense. Paul starts at the beginning and asks Agrippa for patience as he presents his personal history and credentials as a Pharisee.

> "And now I stand here on trial because of my hope in the promise made by God to our fathers, to which our twelve tribes hope to attain, as they earnestly worship night and day. And for this hope I am accused by Jews, O king!" (26:6–7)

Paul is saying that the hope he is preaching is really the same hope Israel has always had—hope in a messiah. The coming of this Messiah would usher in a new age. Satan and evil would be gone for good; the world would enjoy perfect, universal peace and justice. This was the hope that distinguished Israel from all the other nations and religions. The Old Testament scriptures explicitly taught that the messianic age would be inaugurated by the resurrection of the dead (e.g., Dan. 12:2). Paul explains that he had taken hold of this hope when he was a youth and that it is this hope that he continues to hold on to and preach to others. His insinuation is that he believes the same thing the Pharisees believe. If he's on trial for it, maybe they should be on trial too! Paul asks:

"Why is it thought incredible by any of you that God raises the dead?" (26:8)

Paul's question is based on the fact that the Jews have always believed there will be a resurrection from the dead. Yet they've been stubbornly unwilling to accept that God raised Jesus of Nazareth from the dead. Paul's question is that since their hope depends on the power of God to raise the dead, why do they find it so hard to believe he raised this one man from the dead?

What evidence did Paul have that Jesus, in fact, had risen from the dead? Not only were there hundreds of witnesses. He has his own eyewitness testimony (26:12–15). He tells Agrippa the story of how heaven was opened to him as he was on the Damascus road where he saw and heard the resurrected and ascended Jesus speak to him. From that moment on, his commission from the chief priests to persecute Christians was replaced by an altogether different commission from the risen Lord Jesus, who said to him:

"Rise and stand upon your feet, for I have appeared to you for this purpose, to appoint you as a servant and witness to the things in which you have seen me and to those in which I will appear to you, delivering you from your people and from the Gentiles—to whom I am sending you." (26:16–17)

The risen Jesus had a new appointment for Paul. He would no longer be doing the Sanhedrin's bidding. Paul was appointed to be a servant of the risen Jesus. Next, Paul stated exactly what the risen Jesus sent him to do, which clearly had everything to do with salvation by faith and not treason against Caesar. He told them that Jesus had said to him:

"[I am sending you] to open their eyes, so that they may turn from darkness to light and from the power of Satan to God, that they may receive forgiveness of sins and a place among those who are sanctified by faith in me." (26:18)

Ever since Paul saw the risen Jesus and became convinced that Jesus is the first of all who will rise from the dead on the last day, Paul has been wholly given over to the task given to him by Jesus. He's been setting before Jews and Gentiles the truth about who Jesus is and inviting them to open their eyes to see him. He's been calling them to turn away from the darkness of idolatry and unbelief and toward the light of the beauty and goodness of Jesus. He's been calling them to be freed from the powers of Satan that only enslave them and to enjoy the cleansing, healing power of God. He's been showing them how they can receive forgiveness of their sins so that their consciences can be cleansed, and how they can know that they belong to those whom God has set apart to himself for all eternity.

Of course, it is Paul's offering this "place among those who are sanctified" (26:18) to Gentiles that has caused so much friction with the Jews.

"I stand here testifying both to small and great, saying nothing but what the prophets and Moses said would come to pass: that the Christ must suffer and that, by being the first to rise from the dead, he would proclaim light both to our people and to the Gentiles." (26:22–23)

Paul says that the Old Testament says that the Christ would suffer and that he would rise from the dead. He doesn't go into exactly where it says this in the Old Testament. Indeed the whole of the Old Testament testifies to a suffering Savior from the very first time he was promised. Genesis 3:15 says that the offspring of the woman who will put an end to evil will have his heel bruised in the process. He will suffer in accomplishing our salvation. We see shadows of the suffering Savior in Joseph and Job and in so many other people and patterns and prophecies. But we see not only a suffering Savior;

we see a risen Savior, a Savior who defeats death and the grave. God promises to put a son of David on the throne who will rule forever (2 Sam. 7:12–13). He says that the body of this King will not rot in the grave but will live (Ps. 16:10–11). When Isaiah writes about the Lamb led to the slaughter who makes his grave with the wicked, he also says that "when his soul makes an offering for guilt, he shall see his offspring; he shall prolong his days" (Isa. 53:7–12). According to Jesus, we see a preview of his resurrection in the story of Jonah, in the belly of the whale for three days and three nights and then "resurrected" (Jonah 1:17; Matt. 12:40).

As closely as Paul had studied the Old Testament under the rabbis, he hadn't been able to see these things. But then the one who has sent him to open eyes opened his eyes, and he could see clearly that the whole of the Old Testament pointed toward the suffering and glory, the death and resurrection of Jesus.

What Is the Verdict?

Paul has now been imprisoned for over two years. He's had two Roman trials and now this hearing before Agrippa. He deserves a clear verdict. But all he gets is this:

> Then the king rose, and the governor and Bernice and those who were sitting with them. And when they had withdrawn, they said to one another, "This man is doing nothing to deserve death or imprisonment." (26:30–31)

They're willing to say it to each other but not to make it official. They're going to send Paul on to Caesar without any valid charges of a crime against Rome.

While Paul may not have a clear verdict, he does have a clear conscience. Paul has a clear conscience in regard to his faithfulness to the Scriptures. He has a clear conscience in regard to his submission to governing authorities. He has a clear conscience in regard to his obedience to the divine appointment he received from Jesus. He may not be free to go where he pleases, but he has a freedom of soul.

And that freedom of soul is appealing, isn't it?

So let me ask you, how's your conscience these days? Does it nag at you? When? In what situations? One day you and I are going to stand before a judge, a judge with far more authority than those Paul stood in front of. So perhaps it is an important question to ask ourselves: Is my conscience before God clear enough to enter the court of heaven with no fear? Or is there something nagging at my conscience that I just need to 'fess up to? And how about my conscience before man, knowing that, as Paul wrote in Romans 13, "whoever resists the authorities resists what God has appointed, and those who resist will incur judgment" (v. 2)?

There are plenty of people in this world who never think about whether they have a clear conscience. Yet their conscience is there, oftentimes condemning them. Some ruin their lives seeking to silence the inner voice that declares them guilty. But none of us wants an unexamined or silenced conscience. We want a cleansed conscience. And only the death and resurrection of the only person who ever had a perfectly clear conscience is enough to pay the price for all the sin that has sullied our consciences. Because he has loved us enough to take upon himself all of our sin, we know that "if we confess our sins, he is faithful and just to forgive us our sins and to cleanse us from all unrighteousness" (1 John 1:9).

Here's the beautiful thing for the believer: there is no reason not to come clean, because we know there is therefore now no condemnation for those who are in Christ Jesus (Rom. 8:1). We have a ready resource to cleanse our sullied consciences, the blood of Christ. This means we can "draw near with a true heart in full assurance of faith, with our hearts sprinkled clean from an evil conscience and our bodies washed with pure water" (Heb. 10:22). We can say, "My conscience is clean, not because I've never done anything wrong or because I've been able to make the wrong I've done right on my own. My conscience is clean because Jesus has cleansed it with his own blood. His Spirit is at work in me, convicting me of sin so that I can confess it and be cleansed of it. Even more, his Spirit is giving me an ever-increasing desire to be holy as he is holy."

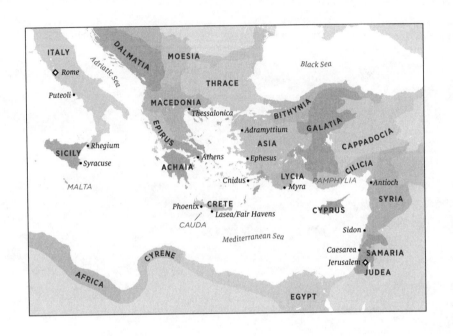

17

It Will Be Exactly as I Have Been Told

Acts 27:1–28:30

RECENTLY DAVID AND I were looking for a place to eat in a city we were visiting. So David looked up some reviews and couldn't resist reading this one to me. (I'm going to change the name of the restaurant to a made-up name.)

There are four types of people who give Star Steakhouse anything higher than two stars.

1. Those on Star Steakhouse's payroll.
2. Those born without taste buds.
3. Those rating the service, not the food.
4. Those who simply feel sorry for Star Steakhouse and never give low ratings.

"Come on down and try our steaks," they say. "We have expensive food, a great atmosphere, and we've been open for decades. We have to be good!" I have never talked to anyone who was satisfied at Star Steakhouse. Everyone I know walked away disappointed, dumbfounded at how they stay in business. The word *steak* is part of their title, and yet these are quite possibly the worst steaks in town. Absolutely flavorless. The cheeseburger, yikes! The salad, uh! The au gratin potatoes, awful! The shrimp and grits, barf! I'd rather eat my way across the lawn than eat this food again!

He had read all the hype and all the restaurant's claims to greatness, but clearly this customer did not find his experience of this restaurant to be everything he was told it would be.

In the first chapter of Acts, Jesus told the apostles how the future would be: "You will receive power when the Holy Spirit has come upon you, and you will be my witnesses in Jerusalem and in all Judea and Samaria, and to the end of the earth" (1:8). In chapter 2 the Holy Spirit came upon them, and they received power. In chapters 2–7 they witnessed about Jesus in Jerusalem. In chapters 8 and 10 they witnessed in Samaria. We read about the appointment of Paul as the apostle to the Gentiles in chapter 9, and then, beginning in chapter 11, the apostolic witness expands to Jews and Gentiles beyond Judea and Samaria, spreading throughout the known world, or "to the ends of the earth." What Jesus said would happen, happened.

If we trace the story of Paul in Acts, we also see that what Jesus said would happen specifically to Paul, happened. Jesus told Ananias that Paul would "carry my name before the Gentiles and kings and the children of Israel" (9:15), and that is exactly what he has done. When he was on trial in Jerusalem, we read, "The Lord stood by him and said, 'Take courage, for as you have testified to the facts about me in Jerusalem, so you must testify also in Rome'" (23:11). Though forty Jews have bound themselves by a pact not to eat or drink until they have killed Paul, Paul is not particularly concerned. Why? He believes that what Jesus said would happen will happen. He will testify to Christ in Rome. This solid confidence carries him through two years under the custody of Felix in Caesarea, the trial before Festus, and the hearing before Agrippa. He doesn't know when or how or exactly what it is going to look like, but because Jesus has said that he will testify to him in Rome, Paul believes that God will get him there.

The whole book of Acts up to this point has been about the saving power of God. So we're not surprised, here at the end of the book, to see the saving power of God at work in every twist and turn of Paul's journey to Rome to assure that God's purposes are accomplished.

Paul Sails for Rome

Acts 27 provides for us a very detailed account of Paul's journey to Rome. Very detailed. Every stop. Every development. He is accompanied by Aristarchus, who has been a companion to him since his days in Ephesus. Evidently Luke is with him as well, as he writes that "we" sailed for Italy (27:1). First, they sailed along the coast of Asia to Lycia. There they boarded a different ship from Alexandria carrying a load of grain and headed for Rome. We know exactly what time of year it was, which was a huge red flag to Paul.

> Since much time had passed, and the voyage was now danger-
> ous because even the Fast was already over, Paul advised them,
> saying, "Sirs, I perceive that the voyage will be with injury and
> much loss, not only of the cargo and the ship, but also of our
> lives." (27:9–10)

It's October, the time of year when cargo ships don't set sail across the Mediterranean because it is getting too close to winter. But this ship is carrying a huge load of grain from Egypt to Rome, where the owner of the grain on board will get a good price if it gets there in time to feed the population of Rome through the winter, so they're anxious to get there. The pilot and the owner of the ship don't want to spend the winter in the little port of Fair Havens (though it sounds like a perfectly lovely place to me), so they put out to sea. At first, we read that "the south wind blew gently" (27:13). But that's about to change.

> But soon a tempestuous wind, called the northeaster, struck down from the land. And when the ship was caught and could not face the wind, we gave way to it and were driven along. (27:14–15)

The wind and waves are taking their toll on the ship, so they wrap cables across and under the center of the ship to try to hold the ship together (27:17). When the storm doesn't let up, they begin to jettison some of the cargo and then some of their equipment (27:18–19).

> When neither sun nor stars appeared for many days, and no small tempest lay on us, all hope of our being saved was at last abandoned. (27:20)

All Hope Is Abandoned

The sailors depend on the sun and the stars to navigate the ship, but they haven't seen sun or stars for many days. It's been day after day of wind and rain on a ship that is barely holding together. They're literally at the end of their rope and have run out of any hope of being saved from the hammering storm and the rocky coastline.

> Since they had been without food for a long time, Paul stood up among them and said, "Men, you should have listened to me and not have set sail from Crete and incurred this injury and loss." (27:21)

(I have to admit that I kind of like this. It's like Paul simply can't resist saying, "I told you so.")

> "Yet now I urge you to take heart, for there will be no loss of life among you, but only of the ship. For this very night there stood before

me an angel of the God to whom I belong and whom I worship, and he said, 'Do not be afraid, Paul; you must stand before Caesar. And behold, God has granted you all those who sail with you.' So take heart, men, for I have faith in God that it will be exactly as I have been told." (27:22–25)

Everything about the circumstances around him says, "Give it up. There's no hope. They're going to find your dead bodies floating on the sea once this storm finally stops." But Paul has heard another voice, and it has said, "Don't be afraid. I've got this. Nobody is going to die. I'm going to get you to Rome to testify to me before Caesar just like I told you." And Paul believes it! Every experience in his life of faith so far has prepared him for this one. Whatever Jesus has said will happen has happened. And so now, he has faith that the outcome of the ship in the storm will be exactly as Jesus has told him it will be.

Paul says, "We must run aground on some island" (27:26). Paul is simply a prisoner catching a ride to Rome on their ship, but the ship's pilot and crew seem to follow his instructions and begin looking for land. In fact, when Paul tells the soldiers guarding him that if some sailors who are trying to get away on the ship's boat (the small boat used to get to land from the large ship) succeed, they won't be saved, the soldiers cut the ropes holding the ship's boat and let it float away. Evidently they're convinced by Paul's confidence in what he's been told by his God.

As day was about to dawn, Paul urged them all to take some food, saying, "Today is the fourteenth day that you have continued in suspense and without food, having taken nothing. Therefore I urge you to take some food. For it will give you strength, for not a hair is to perish from the head of any of you." . . . And when they had eaten enough, they lightened the ship, throwing out the wheat into the sea. (27:33–34, 38)

The only way these 276 people are going to be willing to eat a meal and then throw the rest of their food supply into the sea is if they're convinced that what Paul has told them is true—that this is going to be the day of their salvation and that they're not going to die. If that's true, then they can throw all of the wheat into the sea.

But then everything starts falling apart.

Everything Falls Apart

Now when it was day, they did not recognize the land, but they noticed a bay with a beach, on which they planned if possible to run the ship ashore. So they cast off the anchors and left them in the sea, at the same time loosening the ropes that tied the rudders. Then hoisting the foresail to the wind they made for the beach. But striking a reef, they ran the vessel aground. The bow stuck and remained immovable, and the stern was being broken up by the surf. The soldiers' plan was to kill the prisoners, lest any should swim away and escape. But the centurion, wishing to save Paul, kept them from carrying out their plan. He ordered those who could swim to jump overboard first and make for the land, and the rest on planks or on pieces of the ship. And so it was that all were brought safely to land. (27:39–44)

Everything has literally fallen apart. Some people are swimming to shore. Others are floating on planks and pieces of the ship. If we'd viewed the scene, we'd have been sure that someone was going to die in the process. But no. "All were brought safely to land" (27:44). What Jesus had said would happen has happened. All 276 passengers have been saved from the stormy seas.

After we were brought safely through, we then learned that the island was called Malta. The native people showed us unusual kindness, for they kindled a fire and welcomed us all, because it had begun to rain and was cold. (28:1–2)

It's raining again, and it's cold, but these kind Maltese have kindled a fire for them and made them welcome. Surely Paul lets out a deep sigh of relief. But then things go from bad to worse.

Things Go from Bad to Worse

> When Paul had gathered a bundle of sticks and put them on the fire, a viper came out because of the heat and fastened on his hand. When the native people saw the creature hanging from his hand, they said to one another, "No doubt this man is a murderer. Though he has escaped from the sea, Justice has not allowed him to live." (28:3–4)

Not only has a venomous snake sunk its fangs into Paul's hand; the kind people of Malta have come to the conclusion that anyone who survives a shipwreck only to be bitten by a snake is not just having a bad day but is being punished for a terrible crime. They think that the Roman goddess Justice, who ensured that criminals got what they deserved, has struck Paul through the means of this viper.

> He, however, shook off the creature into the fire and suffered no harm. They were waiting for him to swell up or suddenly fall down dead. But when they had waited a long time and saw no misfortune come to him, they changed their minds and said that he was a god. (28:5–6)

The text doesn't tell us how Paul responded to being called a god, but we should probably assume that he responded the same way he did back in Lystra when people thought he was a god because he healed the man who had never walked. In that instance, he told the people that he was not, in fact, a god, but that they should turn to the living God (14:8–15).

> Now in the neighborhood of that place were lands belonging to the chief man of the island, named Publius, who received us and

entertained us hospitably for three days. It happened that the father of Publius lay sick with fever and dysentery. And Paul visited him and prayed, and putting his hands on him, healed him. And when this had taken place, the rest of the people on the island who had diseases also came and were cured. (28:7–9)

There on Malta, Paul begins to do what has been a mark of the ministry of the apostles whenever they've gone into pagan territory, which is to become a conduit for the power of God that heals and saves.

They also honored us greatly, and when we were about to sail, they put on board whatever we needed. (28:10)

God has not only sovereignly saved their lives; he is sovereignly providing for all their needs through these Maltese, many of whom had likely taken hold of Christ by faith over the three months Paul was there ministering to them.

Just when it seemed that everything was going from bad to worse, Paul, once again, experienced the saving power of God. Not only was he saved from the poisonous snake; he became the conduit of the power of God to heal bodies and save souls in a place where the gospel had not yet been heard.

God's Promises Will Be Kept

After three months we set sail in a ship that had wintered in the island, a ship of Alexandria, with the twin gods as a figurehead. (28:11)

That's an interesting detail, isn't it? Why would Luke tell us about the emblem on this third ship that will finally take Paul and the other 275 people to Rome? Evidently his original readers would have known what the "twin gods" were. "The twin gods were Castor and Pollux,

Greek gods believed to protect sailing ships, provide good winds, and help shipwrecked sailors."[1] Perhaps he wants us to see the irony. We as readers know that it is not these imaginary gods who will assure Paul and the others safe passage to Rome. It is the power of God. Jesus has promised that all 276 will get safely to Rome, and he will keep his promise.

The ship docked at Puteoli (28:13), where a number of believers in Jesus gave Paul, Luke and Aristarchus, and perhaps Julius, his Roman guard, lodging for seven days. Then they headed up the Via Appia, another one of those important Roman roads, toward Rome. But before they could get there, some believers from Rome met them along the way, first in Appius, which was 40 miles from Rome, and then at Three Taverns, which was 12 miles closer to Rome (28:15). Luke writes, "On seeing them, Paul thanked God and took courage" (28:15).

Paul has been on his way to Rome for a long time now. It was way back, near the end of his second missionary journey, when Paul left Ephesus, that he first expressed his intentions to go to Rome (19:21). Throughout his ministry he's been targeting major cities where he has gone to preach the gospel and plant churches that would then take the gospel to their surrounding area. Now he's finally getting to Rome, which is the most major of cities, the Gentile "ends of the earth." As Paul witnesses to the risen Jesus in Rome, Jesus's promise that his apostles would be his witnesses to the ends of the earth is fulfilled.

And we shouldn't be surprised that Paul's witness to Jesus in Rome follows the same pattern it has in every city he has come to. He starts with the Jews (28:17–20), explaining how he had been delivered as a prisoner from Jerusalem even though he had done nothing against the Jewish people or Jewish customs but, in fact, shared the same hope—God's promises being fulfilled through his Messiah—that they had.

---

1   Brian J. Vickers, *John–Acts*, ESV Expository Commentary (Wheaton, IL: Crossway, 2019), 577–78.

And they said to him, "We have received no letters from Judea about you, and none of the brothers coming here has reported or spoken any evil about you. But we desire to hear from you what your views are, for with regard to this sect we know that everywhere it is spoken against." (28:21–22)

I wonder if Paul thought to himself, "Excellent! Here are Jews who don't know anything about all the controversies and conflicts I've had with Jews throughout Macedonia and Syria and Asia and in Jerusalem. They want to hear about 'this sect'? I'll tell them all about the Christ whom Christians have put their faith in. Maybe they'll be able to hear it."

When they had appointed a day for him, they came to him at his lodging in greater numbers. From morning till evening he expounded to them, testifying to the kingdom of God and trying to convince them about Jesus both from the Law of Moses and from the Prophets. And some were convinced by what he said, but others disbelieved. (28:23–24)

The results among the Jews in Rome are the same as he has experienced everywhere that he has presented Jesus as the Christ. Some are convinced. Some refuse to believe.

Paul has a message for those who refuse to believe, using a text they would be familiar with, the text of Isaiah. Isaiah had been commissioned by God to speak his message to people who wouldn't listen. Paul tells the unbelieving Jews in Rome that they are just like those who refused Isaiah's message.

And disagreeing among themselves, they departed after Paul had made one statement: "The Holy Spirit was right in saying to your fathers through Isaiah the prophet:

'Go to this people, and say,
"You will indeed hear but never understand,
    and you will indeed see but never perceive."
For this people's heart has grown dull,
    and with their ears they can barely hear,
    and their eyes they have closed;
lest they should see with their eyes
    and hear with their ears
and understand with their heart
    and turn, and I would heal them.'" (28:25–27)

Paul essentially says, "You're just like your parents who refused to listen to Isaiah's message! You're deaf and blind like they were. You refuse to see that Jesus is the very one you've been looking for and waiting for. You are refusing the salvation of God centered in the person and work of Jesus. So the offer of that salvation is going broader. Your deafness, blindness, and hard-heartedness cannot stop God from gathering a people for himself."

"Therefore let it be known to you that this salvation of God has been sent to the Gentiles; they will listen." (28:28)

Everywhere Paul has gone, the Jews have not wanted to hear Paul say that the offer of God's salvation is going to the Gentiles. The Jews in Rome don't want to hear it either. But that doesn't keep Paul from continuing to offer the salvation of God to all who will listen.

God's Purposes Will Be Accomplished

Paul may be under house arrest in Rome, but the confines of his house can't seem to confine the gospel.

He lived there two whole years at his own expense, and welcomed all who came to him, proclaiming the kingdom of God and teaching about the Lord Jesus Christ with all boldness and without hindrance. (28:30–31)

Paul spent two whole years under house arrest.

If you'd been asked in 2019, "What would you do with a year at home?" most of us would probably have reeled off a number of impressive projects we would accomplish. Then, beginning in March 2020, we got to learn exactly what we would do with a year at home. So we can't help but be impressed with what Paul did with two years under house arrest in Rome. His door was always open. And when people came, he was ready. Jesus had said Paul would take the gospel to Rome, and that is what he did. He's in Caesar's backyard, but he's not holding anything back in regard to proclaiming King Jesus and calling people to bow to him. And nothing is holding him back.

God had a purpose for Paul: *Take the gospel to the Gentiles.* And God had made a promise to Paul: *You will get to Rome.* Paul believed it would be exactly as he had been told, even when all hope had been abandoned, even when all of his resources had run out, even when everything was falling apart, and even when things went from bad to worse.

My friend, God also has a purpose for you. And he has made promises to you. This purpose and these promises provide an anchor for your soul when your circumstances seem hopeless.

When all hope has been abandoned, know that *you* have not been abandoned. You are not a fool to put all of your hope in the promises and purposes of God. His promises will be fulfilled, and his purposes will be accomplished. Jesus's promise to those who endure persecution and even death for his sake is that "not a hair of your head will perish" (Luke 21:18). That promise will be kept. It will be exactly as you have been told.

When everything falls apart, rest in knowing that, really, everything is falling into place. Jesus said, "If I go and prepare a place for you, I will come again and will take you to myself, that where I am you may be also" (John 14:3). It will be exactly as you have been told.

When things go from bad to worse and you think you cannot handle one more hard thing, savor the words of Jesus spoken to Paul after he begged Jesus to take away his pain. "My grace is sufficient. My power is made perfect in weakness" (see 2 Cor. 12:9). Expect that Jesus will be true to this promise. Expect that his grace will be enough to enable you to endure faithfully whatever he has ordained to allow into your life. Expect that his power will be put on display when you have no power to persevere left in yourself.

Have faith in God that everything will be exactly as we have been told throughout the book of Acts. Here are just a few things we've been told:

- Jesus was "the first to rise" (26:23), implying that he won't be the last.

- "Repent and be baptized every one of you in the name of Jesus Christ for the forgiveness of your sins, and you will receive the gift of the Holy Spirit" (2:38).

- "This Jesus, who was taken up from you into heaven, will come in the same way as you saw him go into heaven" (1:11).

- "Everyone who calls upon the name of the Lord shall be saved" (2:21).

It will be exactly as you have been told. Your salvation will not disappoint. There will be no negative reviews. Not only will it be exactly as you have been told; it will be far greater than you can now imagine.

One day, the hope of Israel—a renewed creation, the eradication of evil, a place in the presence of God with perfect security and rest—will no longer be a promise of something out in the future that we put our faith in. Faith will have become sight. We will find ourselves part of a great multitude that no one will be able to number, from every nation, from all tribes and peoples and languages, standing before the throne. We're all going to cry out with a loud voice, "Salvation belongs to our God who sits on the throne, and to the Lamb!" (Rev. 7:10). On that day our glad testimony will be: *All of God's salvation promises have been fulfilled! All of his salvation purposes have been accomplished in my life and in his world. And everything is exactly as I was told.*

Acts Timeline

THE FOLLOWING CHART provides a timeline for key events in the book of Acts. Most of the dates can be determined precisely by correlating biblical events with extensive historical documents and archaeological evidence. Dates with an asterisk denote approximate or alternative dates.

33 (or 30)	Jesus returns to Judea, is crucified and resurrected. James the brother of Jesus becomes a believer after witnessing the resurrected Jesus (Acts 12:17; 1 Cor. 15:7;). Jesus ascends to the Father's right hand (Acts 1). Jesus's first followers receive the Holy Spirit at Pentecost and begin to proclaim the gospel (Acts 2).
33/34*	Paul witnesses the resurrected Lord on the way to Damascus and is commissioned as an apostle to the nations (Acts 9; Gal. 1:15–16).
34–37	Paul ministers in Damascus and Arabia (Acts 9:19–22; 26:20; Gal. 1:16–18).
36/37*	Paul meets with Peter in Jerusalem (Acts 9:26–30; Gal. 1:18).
37–45	Paul ministers in Syria, Tarsus, and Cilicia (Acts 9:30; Gal. 1:21).
38*	Peter witnesses to Cornelius (Acts 10).
41–44	Agrippa, Herod the Great's grandson, rules Palestine; he kills James the brother of John (Acts 12:2) and imprisons Peter (Acts 12:3).

44	Peter leaves Jerusalem; Agrippa is killed by an "angel of the Lord" (Acts 12:23).
44–47*	Paul's second visit to Jerusalem; time of famine (Acts 11:27–30; Gal. 2:1–10).
46–47	Paul's first missionary journey (with Barnabas) from Antioch to Cyprus, Antioch in Pisidia, Iconium, and Lystra (Acts 13:4–14:26).
48*	Paul writes Galatians, perhaps from Antioch (see Acts 14:26–28).
48–49*	Paul and Peter return to Jerusalem for the apostolic council, which, with the assistance of James, frees Gentile believers from the requirement of circumcision in opposition to Pharisaic believers (Acts 15:1–29); Paul and Barnabas return to Antioch (Acts 15:30) but split over a dispute about John Mark (Acts 15:36–40).
48/49–51*	Paul's second missionary journey (with Silas) from Antioch to Syria, Cilicia, southern Galatia, Macedonia, notably Philippi, Thessalonica, and Berea; and then on to Achaia, notably Athens and Corinth (Acts 15:36–18:22).
49	Claudius expels Jews from Rome because of conflicts about Jesus (Acts 18:2); Paul befriends two refugees, Priscilla and Aquila, in Corinth (Acts 18:2–3).
49–51*	Paul writes 1–2 Thessalonians from Corinth (Acts 18:1, 11; also compare Acts 18:5 with 1 Thess. 1:8).
51	Paul appears before Gallio, proconsul of Achaia (Acts 18:12–17).
52–57*	Paul's third missionary journey from Antioch to Galatia, Phrygia, Ephesus, Macedonia, Greece (Acts 18:23–21:17).
52–55	Paul ministers in Ephesus (Acts 19:1–20), writes 1 Corinthians (Acts 19:10).
54	Claudius dies (edict exiling Jews repealed); Priscilla and Aquila return to Rome and host a church in their home (see Rom. 16:3–5).

54–68	Nero reigns.
55–56*	Paul writes 2 Corinthians from Macedonia (Acts 20:1, 3; 2 Cor. 1:16; 2:13; 7:5; 8:1; 9:2, 4; see 1 Cor. 16:5).
57*	Paul winters in Corinth and writes Romans (Acts 20:3; see Rom. 16:1–2; also see Rom. 16:23 with 1 Cor. 1:14), travels to Jerusalem (Acts 21:1–16), visits with James the brother of Jesus (Acts 21:17–26), and is arrested (Acts 21:27–36; 22:22–29).
57–59	Paul is imprisoned and transferred to Caesarea (Acts 23:23–24, 33–34).
60	Paul begins the voyage to Rome (Acts 27:1–2); he is ship-wrecked for three months on the island of Malta (Acts 27:39–28:10).
62*	Paul arrives in Rome and remains under house arrest (Acts 28:16–31); he writes Ephesians, Philippians (Phil. 1:7, 13, 17; 4:22), Colossians (Col. 4:3, 10, 18; see Acts 27:2 with Col. 4:10), and Philemon (see Philem. 23 with Col. 1:7; Philem. 2 with Col. 4:17; Philem. 24 with Col. 4:10; also see Col. 4:9). Luke, Paul's physician and companion (see Col. 4:14), writes Luke and Acts.
62–64	Paul is released, extends his mission (probably reaching Spain), writes 1 Timothy from Macedonia (see 1 Tim. 1:3) and Titus from Nicopolis (Titus 3:12); he is rearrested in Rome (2 Tim. 1:16–17).
64 (July 19)	Fire in Rome; Nero blames and kills many Christians.
64–67*	Paul writes 2 Timothy (see 2 Tim. 4:6–8). Paul and Peter are martyred in Rome.
68	Nero commits suicide; year of the three emperors.
70 (Aug. 30)	Titus, Vespasian's son, after a five-month siege of Jerusalem, destroys the temple after desecrating it; the temple's menorah, Torah, and veil are removed and later put on display in a victory parade in Rome; the influence of the Sadducees ends.

Adapted from the New Testament Timeline in the *ESV Study Bible*. Used by permission.

Bibliography

Beale, G. K., and D. A. Carson. *Commentary on the New Testament Use of The Old Testament.* Grand Rapids, MI: Baker Academic, 2009.

Bruce, F. F., "St. Paul in Macedonia," *Bulletin of the John Rylands University Library of Manchester* 61 (1979): 337–54.

ESV Study Bible. Edited by Wayne Grudem. Wheaton, IL: Crossway, 2011.

Gaffin Jr., Richard B. *In the Fullness of Time: An Introduction to the Biblical Theology of Acts and Paul.* Wheaton, IL: Crossway, 2022.

———. *Perspectives on Pentecost: Studies in New Testament Teaching on the Gifts of the Holy Spirit.* Phillipsburg, NJ: Presbyterian & Reformed, 1979.

Gooding, D. W. *True to the Faith: A Fresh Approach to the Acts of the Apostles.* London: Hodder & Stoughton, 1990.

Johnson, Dennis E. *The Message of Acts in the History of Redemption.* Phillipsburg, NJ: P&R, 1997.

Mote, Justin. "Acts 8–15: City Summer School." Sermon, St. Helen's Bishopsgate City Summer School, July 2007, London. https://www.st-helens.org.uk/.

Schreiner, Patrick. *Acts.* Christian Standard Commentary. Nashville, TN: B&H, 2022.

———. *The Mission of the Triune God: A Theology of Acts.* Wheaton, IL: Crossway, 2022.

Stott, John. *The Message of Acts: To the Ends of the Earth.* The Bible Speaks Today. Downers Grove, IL: IVP Academic, 2020.

Thompson, Alan J. *The Acts of the Risen Lord Jesus: Luke's Account of God's Unfolding Plan.* New Studies in Biblical Theology. Downers Grove, IL: IVP Academic, 2013.

Vickers, Brian J. "Acts." In *John–Acts.* ESV Expository Commentary. Wheaton, IL: Crossway, 2019.

Waters, Guy Prentiss. *A Study Commentary on the Acts of the Apostles.* Louisville, KY: Evangelical Press, 2015.

General Index

Scripture Index

Resources to Go Deeper in Your Study of Acts

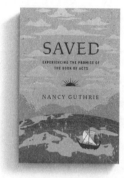

Saved: Experiencing
the Promise of the
Book of Acts

Saved Video Study
(DVD or Download)

Saved Personal
Bible Study
(Paperback or
Printable PDF)

Saved Leader's Guide
(Paperback or
Printable PDF)

ESV Scripture Journal:
Acts (Saved Edition)

For more information, visit **crossway.org**.

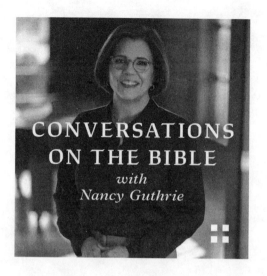

Join bestselling author and speaker Nancy Guthrie in her new podcast as she engages in theologically rich conversations with leading scholars and Bible teachers to deepen our understanding of the Bible.

Subscribe today:

crossway.org/NancyGuthriePodcast